A
JOURNEY
THROUGH
PHILOSOPHY
10 IN 1
ANECDOTES

A
JOURNEY
THROUGH
PHILOSOPHY
1 ⓘ 1
ANECDOTES

NICHOLAS RESCHER

UNIVERSITY OF PITTSBURGH PRESS

Published by the University of Pittsburgh Press, Pittsburgh, Pa., 15260
Copyright © 2015, University of Pittsburgh Press
All rights reserved
Manufactured in the United States of America
Printed on acid-free paper
10 9 8 7 6 5 4 3 2 1

ISBN 10: 0-8229-6335-3
ISBN 13: 978-0-8229-6335-6

Cataloging-in-publication data is on file with the Library of Congress.

CONTENTS

PREFACE

PHILOSOPHY IS, BY TRADITION, the field of inquiry that addresses "the big questions" regarding our human nature and our place in the world's scheme of things.

This book of philosophical anecdotes was written for people who do or might have an interest in philosophy itself, as well as people who like to think about puzzles and paradoxes. In philosophy small-scale problems often bear instructively on large issues. The books most closely akin in spirit to this one are those dealing with philosophically germane puzzles and paradoxes. However, the specifically historical orientation of the present book separates it from such comparable projects.

The reader who takes a particular interest in one of these anecdotes has ample resources, which can easily be located online. There are two excellent informants: *The Internet Encyclopedia of Philosophy* and *The Stanford Encyclopedia of Philosophy*. The problem is not one of sufficiency of information but of a glut. The situation is reminiscent of the lad who asked his mother for information on some subject. She responded "You should really ask your father about that" only to receive the reply "I really don't want to know *that* much about it." To provide the reader some guidelines, each case, each anecdote is fitted out with only a few salient "Further Reading" suggestions. The author is indebted to the publisher's readers for their constructive suggestions and also to Estelle Burris for her patient and painstaking work in putting his manuscript into publishable form.

THEMATIC CLUSTERS

EPISTEMOLOGY

Deceit and Delusion: 11, 36, 39, 97
Demonstration and Substantiation: 7, 8, 38, 57, 63, 87
History and Historicism: 55, 68, 69
Knowledge and Determination: 15, 17, 30, 41, 82, 87
Perspective (Point of View): 3, 9, 66, 83
Principles of Explanation: 5, 6, 8, 10, 22, 23, 27, 45, 51, 57, 63
Skepticism: 22, 36
Subjectivity/Objectivity: 3, 24, 39, 41, 51, 61, 77, 96
Truth: 11, 16, 19, 30, 38, 61, 87

ETHICS AND PHILOSOPHICAL ANTHROPOLOGY

Beauty: 14, 34, 54, 81
Choice and Evaluation: 25, 65, 92, 93, 94
Decision and Action: 2, 3, 24, 80, 93, 94, 87
Evolution: 60, 75, 82
Free Will: 10, 43, 46, 65
Human Nature: 42, 43, 54, 58, 59, 60, 64, 65, 74, 85, 88
Morality and Ethics: 13, 18, 32, 34, 52, 59, 70, 83, 89, 95
Rationality: 2, 61, 77, 91, 93, 97
Trust: 52, 94, 97
Value and Evaluation: 68, 73, 92

LOGIC AND LANGUAGE

Communication: 1, 11, 19, 44, 91, 99, 101
Meaning: 21, 44, 47, 71, 76, 79, 96, 98, 101
Measurement and Quantity: 4, 18, 74, 80
Possibility and Conceivability: 3, 44, 50, 62

A
JOURNEY
THROUGH
PHILOSOPHY
1⊙1
ANECDOTES

INTRODUCTION

WHICH CAME FIRST, the chicken or the egg? All origins are obscure. In the history of primates, just who was the first *Homo sapiens*? And when that baby started babbling, just when was that sound considered its first actual word? In its Greek origin *philosophy* literally means "love of wisdom." But even as people spoke grammatically before there was such a thing as grammar, wisdom had its lovers well before there was any such thing as philosophy. Early on there were various tentative groupings in these directions, but by the time of Plato and Aristotle the discipline was in full swing.

As the idea evolved, philosophy came to address three big themes: the works of nature, the works of humankind, and the endeavor to establish physically and cognitively productive interactions between the two.

The task of the discipline was thus to address "the big questions" regarding humans, the world, and our knowledge of it. Issues of appearance and reality, knowledge and ignorance, and the ramifications of such grand ideas as God and nature, truth and beauty, normality and justice were now on the agenda of deliberation, with the focus on such issues as:

Meaning	How the mechanisms of assertion and discourse work.
Truth	How the truth of our claims is to be substantiated.
Knowledge	How we are to secure information about the past, present, and future.
Value	What sorts of goals, desiderata, and positivities there are for assessing the appropriateness of choices.
Action	What we can do in implementing our decisions.
Ethics	What we should do and how we ought to comport ourselves individually and collectively in relation to ourselves and others.

This is a book of philosophically instructive anecdotes written for philosophically sophisticated thinkers. Even as a mathematical proof consists of a series of small incremental steps of argumentation, so a course of philosophical reasoning and reflection consists of a sequence of considerations each of which is, in principle, sufficiently small in scope and scale to admit of examination in an anecdotal manner. Throughout philosophy's history philosophers have employed little stories that help to make big points. Such anecdotes always issue double invitations: On the one hand they provide an occasion for learning more about the thought and work of the thinkers who act in or react to such anecdotes. And on the other hand they afford an invitation to think for oneself about the issues that are at stake.

Philosophy is a field in which the answer to every question provides the material for yet further questions, and where the prospect and significance of those further questions depend upon their origin. Accordingly, this is a field that calls for attention to historical context. Here more than anywhere else, dealing with the issue effectively demands attention to the history of the field.

The anecdotes presented here illustrate the fact that the adequate handling of big questions sometimes requires an appropriate treatment of small components. In the course of their large discussions, philosophers often tell small stories or confront issues of detail. These minute forays often offer substantive insight into larger projects and frequently prove to be of interest in and of themselves. Examining such episodes conveys a good idea of the scope and range of philosophical concern, and of the variant perspectives for which philosophers over the ages have viewed the issues of their field. Moreover, an anecdote often serves to render vivid and memorable a point whose doctrinal development would otherwise be long and tedious.

An examination of such episodes is likely to leave the reader with the impression that it is easier to pose philosophical questions than to answer them. And this view of the matter seems substantially correct—and certainly so if by "an answer" one understands a question resolution that should pretty obviously be acceptable to anyone and everyone. For philosophical issues are generally of a sort whose resolution depends not just on discovering and acknowledging the relevant substantiating factors but having a prioritization on significant-ranking among them. And at this point different people are bound to take a different line in line with the nature of their experience in relevant matters. In sum, different assessments of the bearing of relevant considerations point in different directions in a way that blocks the way to a one-size-fits-all issue resolution. And this is not to say that individuals cannot establish that a particular answer is rationally right and proper in the context of their own position. (What is at issue here is not an indifferentist's relativism of subjective tastes but rather a rational contextualism of objective experience.)

The anecdotes are here treated chronologically in the birth-order of the authors or subjects who are their prime protagonists. As the reader will soon note, anecdotal matters figure in every area of philosophical concern and interlace with one another to form a network that spans the entire field. This situation is illustrated in the survey of Thematic Clusters in the front matter and by the thematic cross-references at the end of each anecdote.

One of philosophy's most problematic aspects relates to the resources of discourse. Those big questions that are at the core of the enterprise can all be presented with the language resources of ordinary-life discourse. But ultimately technicalities creep in and philosophy understeps a technical region of its own with all sorts of issues and origins in play. With due effort much of this complication is avoidable, but philosophers often don't bother. It sounds more professional and scientific to speak of entities than of beings, of particulars than of items. Some effort has been made to minimize this sort of thing in the present book, but it must be acknowledged that the habits engrained by many years of disciplinary acculturation are hard to shed.

ANTIQUITY
TO 500 AD

THE TOWER OF BABEL

IT IS FITTING TO begin any survey of philosophical encounters with the biblical allegory of the Tower of Babel:

> And the people said, Go, let us build us a city and a tower, whose top may reach unto heaven; and let us make us a name, lest we be scattered abroad upon the face of the whole earth. And the LORD came down to see the city and the tower, which the children of men builded. And the LORD said, Behold, the people is one, and they have all one language; and this they begin to do: and now nothing will be restrained from them, which they have imagined to do. So, let us go down, and there confound their language, that they may not understand one another's speech. So the LORD scattered them abroad from thence upon the face of all the earth: and they left off to build the city. Therefore is the name of it called Babel; because the LORD did there confound the language of all the earth; and from thence did the LORD scatter them abroad upon the face of all the earth.[1]

---

1. Genesis 11:4–9 (King James Version).

This is a good place to begin because it puts up front one of philosophy's most striking facts—the reality of disagreement and absent consensus. Why should this be?

Does the reason perhaps lie in mutual incomprehension, with different philosophers simply talking past one another? This was the view of the English philosopher and historian R. G. Collingwood. As he saw it, different philosophers with discordant philosophical positions occupy separate and disconnected thought worlds. Adherents of conflicting theories literally "talk a different language," so that when one makes an assertion and the other a denial it is not really the same thing that is at issue. As Collingwood wrote:

> If there were a permanent problem P, we could ask "What did Kant, or Leibniz, or Berkeley, think about P?" and if that question could be answered, we could then go on to ask "was Kant, or Leibniz, or Berkeley, right in what he thought about P?" But what is thought to be a permanent problem P is really a number of transitory problems, $P_1, P_2, P_3, \ldots$ whose individual peculiarities are blurred by the historical myopia of the person who lumps them together under the name P.[2]

On this view philosophical disagreement lies in incomprehension: thinkers of different places and times simply discuss different things—that appearance of disagreement about the same matters is an illusion lying in the eyes of the beholder.

But Collingwood's proposition does not square with the reality of things. Philosophers do discuss the same issues: the issues of moral obligation that concerned Kant are the very selfsame ones with which we still grapple today; the problem of free will that concerned Spinoza is the same one that troubled William James. Indeed the very issue that Collingwood addresses—the problem of philosophical discord—is exactly the same issue about which Immanuel Kant long before him deliberated, condemning this situation as "the scandal of philosophy."

---

2. R. G. Collingwood, *An Autobiography* (Oxford: Clarendon, 1939), 69.

Philosophy then is the battlefield for a clash of divergent evaluations and beliefs. And there is ample ground for seeing its conflicts as real disagreements issuing from different priorities and different values. Time and again it emerges that those disputes are not spurious illusions engaged by linguistic incomprehension but rather differences as to priority and weight in the assessment and interpretation of evidentiary considerations. When Machiavelli rejected the significance of morality in international affairs and Kant insisted upon it, they were not discussing different issues in reciprocally incompressible terms. The medieval schoolmen rightly held disputation to be a natural procedure of philosophizing exactly because philosophical positions are inherently debatable. Almost invariably philosophical questions admit of conflicting and yet not wholly implausible alternative responses.

Philosophy is a lot like engineering—albeit engineering with concepts rather than with materials. The airplane of today is a lot more complicated than that of a century ago. So is the automobile. And so is philosophy. For in philosophy as in engineering every "improvement" designed to reduce some problem or other creates further different problems of its own. And in both fields it transpires that perfection is unattainable. We have to do the best we can with the materials at our disposal. None of our resolutions of the issues are free of problems, and with complexity comes disagreement.

Does disagreement serve any constructive purpose? Evidently it can and should. For it provides each participant in a controversy with an incentive to extend and deepen our knowledge in a search for convincing reasons. Coping with reasoned disagreement is clearly a goad to inquiry and precludes yielding too readily to our initial inclinations to identify our options with the uncontestable truth of things.

RELATED ANECDOTES

FURTHER READING

Borges, J. L. "The Library of Babel," a short story originally published in his 1941 collection *El jardín de senderos que se bifurcan* [*The Garden of Forking Paths*]. Buenos Aires: SUR, 1941; republished in its entirety in *Ficciones* (*Fictions*) in 1944.

Cohen, Aver, and Marcelo Darcal, eds. *The Institution of Philosophy: A Discipline in Crisis*. Chicago: Open Court, 1989.

Collingwood, R. G. *An Autobiography*. Oxford: Clarendon, 1939.

Rescher, Nicholas. *The Strife of Systems*. Pittsburgh: University of Pittsburgh Press, 1985.

Rohl, David. *Legend: The Genesis of Civilisation*. London: Century, 1998.

Smith, W. T. *The Evolution of Language*. Cambridge: Cambridge University Press, 2010.

Tomasello, M. *Origins of Human Communication*. Cambridge: MIT Press, 2008.

2

AESOP'S DONKEY

A CANON IS NOT only a contraption that goes "boom" and projects shells—or an official in a cathedral church—but also a list of works accepted as authoritative in a certain field. And while the tales of the Greek fabulist Aesop (ca. 640–ca. 560 BC) do not figure on the established canon of philosophical books, they are nevertheless full of instructive philosophical ideas and lessons and in consequence not infrequently cited in philosophical discussions.

A splendid instance of the philosophically instructive stories we owe to Aesop is his fable about "The Man, the Boy, and the Donkey." It runs as follows:

> Once upon a time an elderly man and his son were going to market with their donkey. As they were walking along by its side, a countryman passed them and said: "You fools, what is a Donkey for but to ride upon?" So the Man put the Boy on the Donkey and they continued on their way. But soon they passed a group of men, one of whom said: "See that selfish lad letting his father walk while he rides." So the Man ordered his Boy to get off, and got on himself. After a short distance they passed

two women, one of whom said to the father, "Shame on you for making your poor son walk while you ride." And so, the Man puzzled about what to do, but at last took his Boy up before him on the Donkey. By this time they had come to the town, and the passersby began to jeer and point at them. When the Man stopped and asked what they were scoffing at they replied: "Aren't you ashamed of yourself for overloading that poor donkey of yours with your hulking son?" The Man and Boy got off and tried to think what to do. After much thought they at last cut down a pole, tied the donkey's feet to it, and raised the pole and the donkey to their shoulders. They went along amid the laughter of all who met them till they came to Market Bridge, when the Donkey, getting one of his feet loose, kicked out and caused the Boy to drop his end of the pole so that the Donkey fell off the bridge, and his fore-feet being tied together he was drowned. "That will teach you," said an old man who had followed them: "Please all, and you will please none."

The first and most obvious lesson here is that there is just no way of pleasing everyone: different people are going to have different opinions about how to proceed in any given situation, and no one resolution among such alternatives is going to satisfy everyone. So what to do?

Perhaps one can manage to minimize dissatisfaction. A look at the situation from the angle of table 1 shows that alternatives (3) and (4) alone contain level 4 rankings. So let us rule them out of contention. And as between (1) and (2) the superiority of (2) stands: the Man/Boy situation being symmetric here, one might as well let the Donkey decide—reflecting that larger truth that what matters is not just voting but who gets to vote.

Table 1. Preference ranking for this alternative			
Alternatives for Riders	Man	Boy	Donkey
(1) only the man	1	3	3
(2) only the boy	3	1	2
(3) both	2	2	4
(4) neither	4	4	1

The situation is also instructive in illustrating the limits of rational decision theory, which will, of course, yield the right output only when one provides the right input. In the end the key operative principles here are—or should be—as follows:

- The interests of people trump those of animals.
- Frail elders can bear strain less well than healthy youths.

Presumably, then, the old man should by rights ride and the lad walk along. The focus on *preferability* rather than mere *preference* makes the approach of the philosopher not something rather different from that of the decision theorist.

And a further lesson also looms in the background. The donkey story is in a way profoundly emblematic of the situation of philosophy. It pivots on the fact that there are several mutually exclusive alternatives: the number of riders on the donkey can be 0, 1, or 2 and that's it. But no matter which alternative is selected, there will be problems and possible objections—no alternative is cost free in this regard. The challenge is to carry out a cost-benefit analysis—not to find an unproblematically cost-free option but to identify that alternative whose balance of assets over liabilities, advantages over disadvantages, plusses over minuses is optional.

Philosophy is much like that. Its issues always admit of alternative resolutions and none of them are without their problems and difficulties. The challenge is not that of finding the flawless resolution but of finding one that is preferable vis-à-vis the risk because its balance of assets over liabilities—of instructiveness over oddity—is an optimal one.

The philosopher's work is thus primarily one of assessment and evaluation. Often—and especially when the issue of modes of living are on the agenda—the philosopher is not called in to identify the alternatives: others (novelists, for example) are often better able to do that. The philosopher's concern is criteriological—to explain and implement the standards that define the reasons for accounting one alternative as better than another. The task is to provide the materials on whose basis one can reasonably decide which side of the question has the strongest case in its favor.

RELATED ANECDOTES

FURTHER READING

There are many excellent—and often beautifully illustrated—editions of Aesop's fables.

Black, Max. *Perplexities: Rational Choice, the Prisoner's Dilemma, Metaphor, Poetic Ambiguity, and Other Puzzles.* Ithaca: Cornell University Press, 1990.

Cahn, Steven M. *Puzzles and Perplexities.* Lanham: Rowman and Littlefield, 2002.

Fisher, Alec. *The Logic of Real Arguments.* 2nd ed. Cambridge: Cambridge University Press, 2004.

3

XENOPHANES'S ANIMAL THEOLOGIANS

THE EARLY GREEK SAGE Xenophanes of Colophon (ca. 575–ca. 490 BC) is known to posterity only through a small handful of brief quotations. The following stands prominent among them: "If oxen and horses and lions had hands and would use them to produce works of art as we men do, then horses would paint the forms of the gods like horses, and oxen like oxen, and would make their bodies in the image of their own different kinds."[1] This little story has many instructive aspects. It marks the introduction of a new conceptual device—a new thought tool—into the realm of philosophical deliberation. For the reasonings at issue here proceed not by a characterization of the real with its descriptive account of facts but rather in terms of the purely speculative projection of an entirely conjectural hypothesis. It is a prime instance of a mode of challenge that has become strikingly prominent in philosophy: "What would you say if . . . ?"

For another thing, Xenophanes's supposition inaugurates the doctrine of relativism: the position that the truth about things—in

---

1.   John Burnet, *Early Greek Philosophy*, 4th ed. (London: A. C. Black, 1930).

this case about the proper foci of worship—lies in the eyes of the beholder or, to be more accurate about it, the types of beholders at issue.

The pivotal idea here is that differently situated viewers will see things from their own point of view. The idea was further elaborated by Xenophanes's younger countryman Protagoras (ca. 490–ca. 420 BC) who taught that "man is the measure of all things, of that which is that it is, and of that which is not that it is not." This again proceeds at the species level, but later more dogmatic thinkers stretched this *species* relativism to a more distinctively *personal* relativism that sees every individual as the arbiter of "their own truth." And of course at that point the very conception of impersonal factuality vanishes into thin air, and we are left with what is often described as the "sophomore relativism" of the declaration "that's just what *you* think."

Xenophanes's perspective turned the biblical account of the man-God relationship on its head. For where the Bible says that God created man in His own image, Xenophanes in effect tells us that man conceived of God in his own image.

Somewhat frustratingly, Xenophanes failed to tell us just what we are to make of his venture into speculation. Is he trying to support that the idea of a god is a mere fiction—something that we humans have made up in our own terms of reference for the sake of comfort in the difficult world that we don't really understand? Or is he trying to tell us that our thought on the matter is deeply inadequate, replete with anthropomorphism that cannot do justice to a creature whose real nature must transcend the man-bound idea that we humans introduce into deliberation on this topic.

In short, was Xenophanes seeking to *degrade* our idea of God or to *elevate* it? Alas, the sources at our disposal fail to tell us—the information we can recover about his thinking is insufficient on this critical point.

RELATED ANECDOTES

FURTHER READING

Armstrong, Karen. *A History of God: The 4,000-Year Quest of Judaism, Christianity, and Islam*. New York: Ballantine, 1994.

Burnet, John. *Early Greek Philosophy*. 4th ed. London: Macmillan, 1930.

Kirk, G. S, J. E. Raven, and M. Schofield. *The Pre-Socratic Philosophers*. 2nd ed. Cambridge: Cambridge University Press, 1983.

Lesher, J. H. *Xenophanes of Colophon*. Toronto: University of Toronto Press, 1992.

PYTHAGORAS'S NUMBERS

THE GREEK PHILOSOPHER PYTHAGORAS (ca. 570–ca. 490 BC) placed mathematics front and center in the field of philosophical deliberation. Aristotle tells us that the "Pythagoreans, seeing that many structures of numbers characterized sensible bodies, supposed real things to be numbers. . . . For the attributes of numbers are present in the musical scale and in the heavens in many other things."[1] As Pythagoras and his school saw it, the ultimate realities of nature are not the transitory sensible items that figure in our everyday experience but the stable and unchanging quantitative regularities that characterize their operations. On such a doctrinal approach it is not Newton's fallen apple but the Law of Gravity that always obeys, along with everything anywhere, that yields us insight into the nature of the real.

This line of thought runs straight through the history of scientific philosophizing down to the present day. One of its most pointed articulations is the oft-cited dictum of the English physicist Lord

---

1. Aristotle, *Metaphysics*, 1090a, 20–25.

Kelvin (1824–1907): "When you can measure what you are speaking about, and express it in numbers, you know something about it; but when you cannot express it in numbers, your knowledge is of a meager and unsatisfactory kind."[2] The idea that only what is quantified can count as real knowledge of reality has been astir from philosophy's earliest days. It is, however, far more often maintained than argued for. There is, after all, no really decisive reason for denying the qualitative dimension of human experience its instructive place in the cognitive scheme of things. The idea that if you can't say it with numbers, then it's not worth saying is hardly defensible. To paraphrase Hamlet: there are more things in heaven and on earth than are dreamt of in mathematical philosophy.

RELATED ANECDOTES

FURTHER READING

Aristotle, *Metaphysics.*

Barnes, Jonathan. *The Pre-Socratic Philosophers.* London: Routledge, 1982.

Heath, T. L. *Greek Mathematics.* 2 vols. Oxford: Clarendon, 1921.

Kahn, C. *Pythagoras and the Pythagoreans.* Indianapolis: Hackett, 2001.

Kirk, G. S., J. E. Raven, and M. Schofield. *The Pre-Socratic Philosophers.* 2nd ed. Cambridge: Cambridge University Press, 1983.

Newman, James R. *The World of Mathematics.* 4 vols. New York: Simon and Schuster, 1956.

---

2. William Thompson, Lord Kelvin, *Popular Lectures and Addresses* (London: Macmillan, 1891–1894), 1: 73.

5

HERACLITUS'S RIVER

THE GREEK PHILOSOPHER HERACLITUS of Ephesus
(ca. 540–480 BC) was famous even in his own day for the obscurity
of his aphorisms. While only some hundred of his dicta survive,
they have forever secured his reputation as the prophet of change,
transiency, and the impermanence of things. Diogenes Laertius reports on his ideas as follows:

> Fire is the element, all things are exchanged for fire and come
> into being by rarefaction and condensation; but of this he gives
> no clear explanation. All things come into being by conflict of
> opposites, and the sum of things flows like a stream. Further,
> all that is is limited and forms one world. And it is alternately
> born from fire and again resolved into fire in fixed cycles to all
> eternity, and this is determined by destiny. Of the opposites that
> which tends to birth or creation is called war and strife, and that
> which tends to destruction by fire is called concord and peace.
> Change he called a pathway up and down, and this determines
> the birth of the world.[1]

---

1. Diogenes Laertius, *Lives of the Eminent Philosophers*, trans. R. D. Hicks
    (Cambridge: Harvard University Press, 1925), book 9, sects. 6–7.

Although fire was the archetypical element in Heraclitus's theory of nature, water was his most famous analogy, and he will ever be known as the author of the famous "you cannot step into the same river twice" epigram: "Different waters even flow upon those stepping into the same river . . . they scatter and combine . . . converge and diverge . . . approach and depart."[2]

Heraclitus is thus the seer of transiency, echoing his older contemporary, the poet Simonides of Cos, who saw all worldly things as subject to the knowing of the "tooth of time." In maintaining his doctrine of the transiency of all worldly things, Heraclitus deeply influenced Plato and his entire tradition.[3] And this position is also reflected in the Pythagorean ideal of purely abstract mathematics, whose truths claim that the world's things are eternal and indestructible. This contrast between the material and thereby impermanent and the immaterial and thereby permanent exerted a powerful formative influence throughout Western thought.

RELATED ANECDOTES

FURTHER READING

Burnet, John. *Early Greek Philosophy*. 4th ed. London: Macmillan, 1930.
Hahn, Charles H. *The Art and Thought of Heraclitus*. Cambridge: Cambridge University Press, 1981.
Hodge, David, and Hi-Jin Hodge. *Impermanence*. Lanham: Snow Lion, 2009.
Kirk, G. S., J. E. Raven, and M. Schofield. *The Pre-Socratic Philosophers*. 2nd ed. Cambridge: Cambridge University Press, 1983.

---

2. G. S. Kirk, J. E. Raven, and M. Schofield, *The Pre-Socratic Philosophers*, 2nd ed. (Cambridge: Cambridge University Press, 1983), 195.
3. See Plato, *Theaetetus* 152E1; *Cratylus*, 401D5.

6

ANAXIMANDER'S EARTH

THE ANCIENT GREEK THEORIST Anaximander of Miletus (ca. 510–ca. 450 BC) was among the founding fathers of the geocentric theory of the universe. But of course if—as he and most ancients came to believe—the earth is at the center of things in space, the question at once arises: What is it that keeps it firmly fixed in place? Already available here was the old Indian theory that the earth was supported by resting on the back of a large cosmic elephant. But what then of that elephant itself? Some apparently suggested that it stood on a tortoise, which in its turn stood on the back of an alligator. (Humorously, there might be "alligators all the way down.")

For reasons readily understood, Anaximander rejected this sort of solution and offered a different explanation. Here Aristotle gives the following report: "There are some who say, like Anaximander among the ancients, that it [the earth] stays still because of its equilibrium. For it behoves that which is established at the centre, and is equally related to the extremes, not to be borne one whit more either up or down or to the sides; and it is impossible for it to move simultaneously in opposite directions, so that it stays fixed by necessity."[1]

---

1. Aristotle, *De caelo*, II 13, 295b10–13.

Anaximander's solution pivoted on an idea that has a profound hold on the philosophy of ancient Greece and ever since, namely, what came to be known as the principle of sufficient reason. The pivotal idea here is that the universe is a rational place and that whatever is the case about it admits (at least in principle) of a reason for its being so. And rather than opting for some clumsy mechanical resolution, Anaximander put this rational principle to work. If the universe is effectively symmetric, then there could be no further reason—or explanation—for going up rather than down, right rather than left. So then a centrally placed object is bound to remain in place, stably fixed there not by physical machinations but by the rational symmetry of things.

Thus, there emerges the basic lesson that the explanation of things need not be mechanical: rules, laws, and practices can also do the job. Clearly there is here a significant advance in understanding the nature of explanation itself—one which is predicated on the possibility of accounting for aspects of nature not in terms of causal mechanisms but rather in terms of other noncausal but still rationally cogent explanatory principles.

RELATED ANECDOTES

FURTHER READING

Aristotle. *De cealo* [On the Heavens]. The most accessible version is that of W. D. Ross in the Oxford translation of *The Works of Aristotle*. Oxford: Clarendon, 1908.

Burnet, John. *Early Greek Philosophy*. 4th ed. London: Macmillan, 1930.

Kahn, Charles H. *The Art and Thought of Heraclitus*. Cambridge: Cambridge University Press, 1981.

Kirk, G. S., J. E. Raven and M. Schofield. *The Pre-Socratic Philosophers*. 2nd ed. Cambridge: Cambridge University Press, 1983.

Lederman, Leon, and C. T. Hill. *Symmetry and the Beautiful Universe*. Amherst: Prometheus Books, 2005.

Pruss, Alexander R. *The Principle of Sufficient Reason*. Cambridge: Cambridge University Press, 2006.

7

ZENO'S RACES

ZENO (CA. 490–CA. 420 BC) was a leading member of what has become known as the Eleatic school of early Greek philosophy (named after the town of Elea, Zeno's native place). A central teaching of this school was that reality is something very different from the realm of appearance, as we have it in everyday experience. And in particular they held that change and process as we experience them are mere illusions and ultimate reality is itself something fixed and unchanging.

In support of this view, Zeno developed a series of ingenious arguments to the effect that motion is something that is ultimately unintelligible because it is bound to lead to inherent contradictions. Zeno supported this position by several vivid illustrations. One of these became known as "The Stadium" and went as follows:

> Achilles cannot win in a race with the tortoise. Indeed he will not even be able to get started. For to get from the starting point to a farther point out, he would first have to get to the halfway mark to there, and before that he would first have to get to the halfway mark of the halfway mark, and so on *ad infinitum*. But one can never reach an infinite number of points in a finite time.

Nor would Achilles ever be able to finish the race. For to get to the end he would first have to get to the halfway point, and to do this he would have to reach the halfway mark to there, and so on *ad infinitum*. But one can never reach an infinite number of points in a finite time.[1]

A promising way to defeat this reasoning rejects its key premise that one cannot manage to complete an infinite series of steps in a finite period of time, maintaining that (for example) the person who effects a transit from point *A* to point *B* manages to do just exactly that. Of course this could not possibly be accomplished if the agent were to spend any amount of time at each of these intermediate points—if those steps involved processes of some duration in time. But passing through them as way stations en route to a further destination does not require any period of time whatsoever: it can be instantaneous. Stops take time but transits do not. And an infinite number of such accomplishments can indeed be fitted into a finite amount of time, seeing as they are instantaneous.

Zeno's ingenious but flawed argument carries a number of important lessons. The first of them is that outright inconsistency is unacceptable: rational cogency requires consistency. And the second clear lesson now emerges from the fact that contradiction arises in the situation at issue if all of the four following claims were conceded:

(a) Running a race requires completing an infinite number of steps.
(b) Each of these steps invokes a distinct task.
(c) It is impossible to complete infinitely many tasks in a finite amount of time.
(d) Running a race in a finite amount of time is possible.

To restore consistency among these incompatible contentions at least one of these must be sacrificed. The third lesson is that the contradiction contemplated here can be averted by drawing some appropriate distinctions. In particular it should be noted that the inconsistency at issue can be overcome by a distinction between accomplishing distinct steps (which need involve no lapse in time)

---

1. For this paradox, as well as others proposed by Zeno, see Wesley C. Salmon, *Zeno's Paradoxes* (Indianapolis: Bobbs-Merrill, 1970).

and performing distinct tasks (which always require some period of time). And now with this distinction at hand premise (b) of the argument to inconsistency is averted.

To be sure, there is an important point to Zeno's worries about time and process. Our statements about occurrence seem to fix them in time and the fluidity of ever-changing process is hard to capture in language.

Zeno's paradox thus affords a far-reaching methodological lesson, namely, that situations of approaching inconsistency can elicit a philosophical deliberation and that driving distinction affords an effective and substantive means of coping with the problem of consistency and restoration that becomes unavoidable here. His arguments against motion substantiated Zeno's dedication to a larger program of early Greek philosophy, based on the theory that reason reveals to us that the reality of things differs radically from the appearances that our human experiences of the world put at our disposal. For nothing is a more striking feature of our experience than ongoing change and motion. But if this cannot be real because of its inherent contradictions, then the reality that underlies this experience of ours must be something very different from what that experience itself represents it as being. For reason requires that reality itself must be cohesively self-consistent—a nonnegotiable axiomatic commitment of all Greek philosophizing that equally holds for us as well.

RELATED ANECDOTES

FURTHER READING

Hawley, Katherine. *How Things Persist*. Oxford: Oxford University Press, 2001.

Heath, T. L. *Greek Mathematics*. vol. 1, especially chap. 7, 271–83. Oxford: Clarendon, 1921.

Kirk, G. S., J. E. Raven, and M. Schofield. *The Pre-Socratic Philosophers*. 2nd ed. Cambridge: Cambridge University Press, 1983.

Rescher, Nicholas. *Paradoxes*. Chicago: Open Court, 2001.

Salmon, Wesley C. *Zeno's Paradoxes*. Indianapolis: Bobbs-Merrill, 1970.

8

THE ATOMISTS' NATURE

THE GREEK PHILOSOPHER LEUCIPPUS of Miletus (ca. 470–ca. 380 BC) and his younger contemporary Democritus of Abdera (ca. 460–ca. 370 BC) were the founding fathers of Greek atomism, the theory that all that there is in the physical world is nothing but atoms and the void: a vast manifold of imperceptibly minute and hard material particles moving about in empty space. And, as the ancient Greek philosophical historian Aetius tells it, these thinkers taught that, while various theorists conceded reality to the things of the world of sense, the atomists regarded all this as a matter of human thought artifice: "Many hold that the things of sense exist by Nature (*phusis*). But Leucippus and Diogenes have it that such things exist only by Convention (*nomôs*)."[1]

From the outset of Western philosophizing there have been doctrinal conflicts regarding the constitution of reality and the boundary between what is actually real and what is merely a matter of how things appear to us humans. And here the most prominent and persistent position has been that of the materialistic physical-

---

1.   John Burnet, *Early Greek Philosophy*, 4th ed. (London: Macmillan, 1930), 347.

ism inaugurated by these Greek atomists to the effect that it is the world's material, physical, sense-accessible things that are real, and the qualitative realm of our experience is merely a matter of seeming—of how things appear to us. For what alone is real, so the atomists taught, is a range of being entirely outside the domain of human experience: those imperceptibly small material atoms distributed throughout an unendingly vast and otherwise wholly void and empty space. All the rest of it—the totality of the sensible qualities and objects of our experience—is simply a matter of how these basic realities appear to us. Our humanly experienced "reality" is not actually real but only accepted as such on the basis of the experience-guided conceptions we adopt from convenience for our practical purposes.

Accordingly those atomist philosophers put thinking people on notice that deep inquiry shows that reality is something very different from what we standardly take it to be. A correct view of the world will have to be something decidedly different from what the average uninformed human takes it to be. By the time that the natural sciences came to take this position, the philosophers had long accustomed us to it. The "naïve realism" of the doctrine that things are as they appear to be had by then fallen on hard days.

RELATED ANECDOTES

FURTHER READING

Burnet, John. *Early Greek Philosophy*. 4th ed. London: Macmillan, 1930.

Kirk, G. S., J. E. Raven, and M. Schofield. *The Pre-Socratic Philosophers*. 2nd ed. Cambridge: Cambridge University Press, 1983.

Melsen, Andrew G. van. *From Atomos to Atom*. New York: Dover, 1952.

Pyle, Andrew. *Atomism and Its Critics: From Democritus to Newton*. Bristol: Thoemmes, 1997.

Taylor, C. C. W. *The Atomists*. Toronto: University of Toronto Press, 1999.

9

THE ATOMISTS' WORLDS

WITH DEMOCRITUS (CA. 460-CA. 370 BC) most prominent among them, the so-called atomists of ancient Greece envisioned infinite space containing an infinitude of diverse worlds. On this basis they propounded a radical *dissolution* of the problem of unrealized possibilities. On their teaching, unrealized possibilities are an illusion—the "unrealized" possible sun twice as large as ours does in fact exist, albeit in another world located elsewhere in infinite space. There are no nonexistent possibilities: all possibilities are somehow extant, and reality accommodates all possibilities for such alternatives through spatial distribution in different regions: "There are innumerable worlds, which differ in size. In some worlds there is no sun and moon, in others they are larger than in our world, and in others more numerous. The intervals between the worlds are unequal; in some parts there are more worlds, in others fewer; some are increasing, some at their height, some decreasing. . . . They are destroyed by collision one with another. There are some worlds devoid of living creatures or plants or any moisture."[1]

---

1. G. S. Kirk, J. E. Raven, and M. Schofield, *The Pre-Socratic Philosophers* (Cambridge: Cambridge University Press, 1957), 411.

What we have, in effect, is a "many worlds" theory whose every (suitably general) possibility is realized in fact someplace or other. Any alternative possibility for *this* world (i.e., this local *cosmos* of ours) is realized by another world in another region of infinite space. The "nonexistent" possibilities do in fact exist: they just exist elsewhere. On this basis, confronting the question of "Why do dogs not have horns: just why is the theoretical possibility that dogs be horned not actually realized?" the atomists replied that it indeed is realized but just elsewhere—*in another region of all-embracing space.* Somewhere within this infinite manifold, there is another world just like ours in every respect save one: that its dogs have horns. That dogs lack horns is simply a parochial idiosyncrasy of the particular local world in which we interlocutors happen to find ourselves. Reality accommodates all possibilities of worlds alternative to this through spatial distribution: as the atomists saw it, *all* alternative possibilities are in fact actualized in the various subworlds embraced within one spatially infinite superworld. To be sure, while conditions in that other world may differ radically from our own (their dogs may have horns!), there is nothing about such remote world regions that is inconsistent or incompatible with all that exists and happens in ours.

Various Greek theorists since Parmenides worried about how meaningful discussion about unreal possibilities is feasible. The atomists had a simple solution here: there just aren't any because all possibilities are realized. And of course this theory of many worlds also led to questions of their nature and to speculation about alien life forms that continues to the present day.

RELATED ANECDOTES

FURTHER READING

Barnes, Jonathan. *Early Greek Philosophy*. New York: Penguin, 1987.

Dick, Steven J. *Plurality of Worlds*. Cambridge: Cambridge University Press, 1982.

Kirk, G. S., J. E. Raven, and M. Schofield. *The Pre-Socratic Philosophers*. 2nd ed. Cambridge: Cambridge University Press, 1983.

10

SOCRATES'S
DISAPPOINTMENT

IN PLATO'S DIALOGUE *PHAEDO*, Socrates (450–399 BC),
Plato's primary spokesman, tells the following story:

> I learned that a book by Anaxagoras said that mind is really
> the arranger and cause of all things. I was delighted with this
> explanation, and it seemed to me in a certain way to be correct
> that mind is the cause of all, and I thought that if this is true,
> mind arranging all things places everything as it is best . . . I
> thought he would show me first whether the earth is flat or round
> . . . and if he said it was in the middle of the universe, he would
> proceed to explain how it was better for it to be in the middle;
> . . . But as I went on reading I saw Anaxagoras using mind not at
> all and stating no valid causes for the arrangement of all things,
> but giving airs and ethers and waters as causes and many other
> strange things. I felt very much as I should feel if someone said,
> "Socrates does by mind all he does," and then trying to tell the
> causes of each thing I do, if he should say first that the reason
> why I sit here now is that my body consists of bones and sinews,
> and the bones are hard and have joints between them, and the
> sinews can be tightened and slackened . . . and make me able

to bend my limbs now, and for this cause I have bent together and sit here; and if next he should give you other such causes of my conversing with you, alleging as causes voices and airs and hearings and a thousand others like that, and neglecting to give the real causes.[1]

Socrates's complaint about Anaxagoras set the stage for a far-reaching and enduring controversy in the history of Western philosophizing. For it inaugurated the conflict between those who seek to explain the world's occurrences and arrangements on the sole basis of physical causality and those who envision an explanatory role for principles of normative rationality. For in contrast to the physicalistic tradition of Anaxagoras, there stands the fundamentally finalistic tradition of the Platonic school of thought regarding the rationality of the real. After all, the physical causality approach to nature, while quite effective in explaining *how* things happen in the world, remains in embarrassed silence on the question of *why* things happen in this way. (Leibniz in the seventeenth century sought to reconcile the two by proposing that, while occurrences can and should be explained physicalistically in terms of the physical laws of nature, these laws themselves can and should be accounted for functionally and functionalistically.)

The controversy continues to the present day and figures at two levels. One is the localized level of human agency—are we humans merely complex machines or has a new mechanism-transcending capacity emerged in the course of our evolution? And the other is the global level of the development and constitution of the cosmos—is this the product of the feckless interplay of natural forces or is it a matter of intelligent design, the fruit not necessarily of a designer but at any rate of some force or agency that operates so as to instill order, harmony, and rational coherence into the world's arrangements?

So in one way or another conflict between material causality and rationalistic teleology has pervaded the entire history of philosophy. It is, however, neither accurate nor just to characterize the former position as *naturalism*, as is so often done. For teleologists do

---

1. Plato, *Phaedo*, 97D–99D.

not deny those physical operations in nature but simply have a different view regarding what is natural, regarding the telic impetus to rational economy and order as an inherent feature of the world's natural modus operandi.

RELATED ANECDOTES

FURTHER READING

Carlo, Mario de, and David MacArthur, eds. *Naturalism and Normativity*. New York: Colombia University Press, 2010.

Plato. *Phaedo*. There are various excellent translations of Plato's dialogues, this one included: Bostock, David. *Plato's* Phaedo. Oxford: Clarendon, 1986. This edition contains helpful commentary.

Wallis, W. T., and Jay Bregman. *Neo-Platonism and Gnosticism*. Albany: SUNY Press, 1992.

Whittaker, Thomas. *The Neo-Platonists*. Cambridge: Cambridge University Press, 1901.

11

EUBULIDES'S RIDDLE AND EPIMENDES'S LIE

I CANNOT COHERENTLY MAINTAIN "my belief that p is the case is a false belief" because the second part of this statement contradicts the first. But I can assuredly and unproblematically maintain "Jones's belief that p is the case is a false belief." My having the false belief is not just a possibility but doubtless an actual fact. Yet nevertheless the predicate "_____ is a false belief of mine" is something I cannot possibly instantiate with respect to a specifically identified belief.

Concern for logical problems of self-reference first originated with the liar riddle (*pseudomenos*) of the Greek dialectician Eubulides of Megra (ca. 440–ca. 380 BC). He posed the following puzzle: "Does the man who says 'I am lying' actually lie?"[1] The problem at issue was articulated via the following dilemma: The declaration

---

1. Aristotle, *Sophistical Refutations*, 180a35; *Nicomachaean Ethics*, 1146a71. "Si dicis te mentiri verumque dicis, mentiris [If you say that you are a liar and tell the truth, you are a liar]" (Cicero, *Academica priora*, II, 30, 96; and compare, *De divinatione*, II, 11). Or consider the question of whether the witness who declares "I am perjuring myself" does actually do so in making this assertion.

that I lie will be either true or false. But if this declaration is true, then I lie, and my declaration will be false. But if that declaration is false, then what it says—namely, that I lie—is not the case and I must be speaking the truth. Thus either way the truth status being assigned is inappropriate.

What we have here is a self-falsifying statement that involves an inherent conflict of truth claims. For if we accept the contention at issue as true, then it itself will have to be false so that the statement implies its own negation.

Eubulides's riddle was popular in classical antiquity.[2] And it gave rise to the puzzle of the ancient story of Epimendes the Cretan, who is supposed to have said that "All Cretans are liars"— with "liar" being understood in the sense of a *congenital* liar," someone incapable of telling the truth. (To be sure, if by "liar" one meant someone who lies frequently, but not always, there would be nothing paradoxical about the "liar" paradox.)

Such situations of self-contradiction carry the instructive lesson that self-criticism can clearly go only so far. The people who proclaim themselves unreliable probably are so—but for that very reason we cannot justifiably take them to be so on the present occasion.

RELATED ANECDOTES

71. Frege's Morning Star   202
98. Vagrant Predicates   273

FURTHER READING

Baroise, Jon, and John Etchemende. *The Liar.* Oxford: Oxford University Press, 1987.
Beall, J. C., ed. *Liars and Heaps: New Essays on Paradox.* Oxford: Clarendon, 2003.
Gardner, Martin. *Aha! Gotcha!* San Francisco: W. H. Freeman, 1982.
Rescher, Nicholas. *Paradoxes.* Chicago: Open Court, 2001.

---

2. It not only was discussed by Aristotle and Cicero but in medieval times became a staple in the extensive discussions of insolubilia.

12

PLATO'S *REPUBLIC*

THE REPUBLIC OF THE great Greek philosopher Plato (428–347 BC) is not only the first really substantial philosophical work but also one of the very greatest. It covers an impressive array of topics: the nature of justice and virtue, truth and knowledge, the realm of ideas, the good of persons, the proper organizations of public affairs.

In relation to statecraft, Plato was unabashedly a paternalistic elitist. As he saw it, the public affairs of a city-state should be managed by a carefully trained and selected class. As Plato saw it in *The Republic*, good government is less a matter of laws than of the men charged with the management of affairs. Accordingly, he contemplated the establishment of an elite class of carefully selected and trained guardians of the state from among whom, when duly matured and tested by experience, the group of rulers would be constituted. The guardians must be trained to develop both the harder, soldier side of their nature and the softer, cultural side:

> We must choose out of the guardians men such as those whom we observe to be most careful for us all their lives long; who do with all their hearts whatever they think will be for the advantage of the city. . . . They must be watched from childhood up; we must

set them tests in which a man would be most likely to forget such a resolution or to be deceived, and we must choose the one who remembers well and is not easily deceived, and reject the rest. . . . Then whoever is thus tested among boys, youths, and men, and comes out immaculate, he must be established as ruler and guardian of the city; honours must be given him while he lives, and at death public interment and then magnificent memorial. . . . These rulers shall keep watch on enemies without and friends within; they shall see to it that the friends will not wish to injure, and the enemies shall not be able.[1]

Political thought over the centuries has revolved around the issue of the relative priority of the laws that canalize the public affairs and the men who operate them. No one would disagree that good laws with good men is a very good thing, and bad laws with bad men a very bad one. But what of those mixed cases? Some think that the laws are primary: that good laws will automatically ensure the selection of good men to operate them. (Thomas More inclined to this view.) Others think that if good men are in charge, the desideratum of good laws will thereby be provided for. But still others envision a potential for real conflict here and would accordingly place prime emphasis on one side or the other—either the laws (Montesquieu) or the men who have to govern under their aegis (Thomas More).

RELATED ANECDOTES

31. Machiavelli's *Prince* **92**
33. More's *Utopia* **100**
35. Hobbes's *Leviathan* **106**
48. Mandeville's Bees **143**

FURTHER READING

Annas, Julia. *An Introduction to Plato's* Republic. Oxford: Oxford University Press, 1981.

Plato. *The Republic.* Many good translations of Plato's dialogues exist, *The Republic* included; see, e.g., Daryl H. Price, *A Guide to Plato's* Republic (Oxford: Oxford University Press, 1998); Greg Recco, *Athens Victorious: Democracy in Plato's* Republic (Lanham: Lexington, 2007); and Sean Sayers, *Plato's* Republic: *An Introduction* (Edinburgh: Edinburgh University Press, 1999).

---

1. Plato, *The Republic*, 412B–44B.

13

PLATO'S RING OF GYGES

IN BOOK II OF *The Republic*, Plato uses the story of a magic ring to illustrate the benefits of moral comportment:

> This licence I have spoken of is much the same as the power which the shepherd Gyges had, the ancestor of Gyges the Lydian. . . . It was the custom among the shepherds to hold a monthly meeting, and then report to the king all about the flocks; this meeting he attended wearing the ring. As he sat with the others, he happened to turn the collet of the ring round towards himself to the inside of his hand. As soon as this was done he became invisible to the company, and they spoke of him as if he had left the place. He was surprised, and fingered the ring again, turning the collet outwards, and when he turned it he became visible. Noticing that, he made trial of the ring, to see if it had that power; and he found that whenever he turned the collet inside, he was invisible, when he turned it outside, visible. After he found this out he managed to be appointed one of the messengers to the king; when he got there, he seduced the king's wife, and with her set upon the king, and killed him, and seized

the empire. . . . It was in his power to take what he would even out of the market without fear, and to go into any house and lie with anyone he wished, and to kill or set free from prison those he might wish, and to do anything else in the world like a very god. And in doing so he would do just the same as the other; both would go the same way. Surely one would call this a strong proof that no one is just willingly but only under compulsion.[1]

Here Socrates confronted the challenge: What actual individual could—and what sensible individual would—resist an opportunity to obtain illicitly the manifold goods of this world if he was sure of getting away with it scot-free? What is basically at issue here is a dual vision of man and the human condition at large, one that sees us in the dual perspective of what we are and what we ought to be—of what is *seemingly* and *superficially* in our interests and what is *actually* and *fundamentally* so.

And so Socrates had a good reply at the ready. For as he sees it, that malefactor does not really manage to "get away with it." For the evildoer is ultimately caught and punished—by themself. For he or she knows what has been done, and thereby a real price is paid. The malefactor can no longer look in the mirror and claim to be seeing an honest person. The individual's very actions here condemned them and imposed the penalty: a loss of claims to self-respect.

The Ring of Gyges story exemplifies a particularly pervasive and prominent type of philosophical issue, namely, a conflict of values. For it highlights a clash between two important value interests of ours, namely, *self-respect* on the one hand and *material benefit* on the other. And after an in-depth examination of the complex composition of the human psyche (the "parts of the soul") and how they are relished and regulated, the *Republic* ends in comparing the distorted life of the self-seeking tyrant (Gyges) with that of the harmonious and well-ordered life of the philosopher—to the decided advantage of the latter.

And so the story of Gyges's ring conveys a significant philosophical lesson. The actions we perform have a double aspect. They will influence how the world sees us—which is something we may

---

1. Plato, *The Republic*, in *Great Dialogues of Plato*, trans. W. H. D. Rouse (New York: Signet, 1984), 359B–360C.

be able to manipulate. But like it or not, they are also determinative factors of our self-constitution, serving to make us into the sort of persons we in fact are.

RELATED ANECDOTES

FURTHER READING

Crombie, I. M. *Plato's Doctrines*. 2 vols. London: Routledge, 1963.

Irwin, Terence. *Plato's Ethics*. New York: Oxford University Press, 1995.

Lodge, R. C. *Plato's Ethical Theory*. New York: Hardcourt Brace, 1928.

Plato, *The Republic*. There are various good translations of Plato's dialogues, *The Republic* included; see, for example, Plato, *The Republic*, in *Great Dialogues of Plato*, trans. W. H. D. Rouse (New York: Signet, 1984).

14

PLATO'S DEMIURGE

IN HIS DIALOGUE *TIMAEUS*, Plato envisioned four key factors as functioning in the constitution of the cosmos: a primal *Chaos* that operates in an anarchic (literally *lawless*) way under the aegis of a constraining *Necessity*, and a ruling *Creative Power* or *Craftsman* (*Demiurge*) that operates under the direction of *Intelligence* (*nous*, Reason). This last, Intelligence gradually over the course of time "persuades" (!) Necessity to admit the lawful regularity needed to transform Chaos into an orderly cosmos. On this basis it transpires that the Intelligence that guides the operations of the creative demiurge

> is the supremely valid principle of becoming and of the order
> of the world. . . . Desiring then that all things should be good
> and, so far as might be, nothing imperfect, the demiurge
> took over all that is visible—not at rest, but in discordant and
> unordered motion—and brought it from disorder into order,
> since he judged that order was in every way the better. Now
> it was not, nor can it ever be, permitted that the work of the
> supremely good should be anything but that which is best.

Taking thought, therefore, he found that, among things that are by nature visible, no work that is without intelligence will ever be better than one that has intelligence, when each is taken as a whole, and moreover that intelligence cannot be present in anything apart from soul. In virtue of this reasoning, when he framed the universe, he fashioned reason within soul and soul within body, to the end that the work he accomplished might be by nature as perfect as possible.[1]

But Intelligence does not have it all its own way. It must continually contend with Necessity.

Now our foregoing discourse . . . has set forth the works wrought by the labors of Intelligence; but we must now set beside them the things that come about of Necessity. For the generation of this universe was a mixed result of the combination of Necessity and Intelligence which overruled Necessity by persuading her to guide the greatest part of the things that become towards what is best. In this way and on this principle this universe was fashioned in the beginning by the victory of reasonable persuasion or Intelligence over Necessity.[2]

For Plato, cosmology is witness to the development of a largely (but not perfectly) orderly law-governed cosmos out of a confused primal chaos under the pervasive influence of reason. What emerges in the end is a systemic order instituted by the cosmic intelligence of creative focus to provide an existential manifold that is congenial to the finitely intelligent (and thus limitedly rational) beings that emerge within it.

Plato's Pythagoras-inspired conception of a rationally instituted lawfulness transforming a primal chaos into a (largely) orderly cosmos has exerted an enormous influence throughout the subsequent history of Western, scientific, philosophical, and theological thought.

---

1. Plato, *Timaeus*, in *Plato's Cosmology: The* Timaeus *of Plato*, trans. F. M. Cornford (London: Routledge, 1937), 29D–30B.

2. Plato, *Timaeus*, 47E–48B.

RELATED ANECDOTES

FURTHER READING

Broadie, Sarah. *Nature and Diversity in Plato's* Timaeus. Cambridge: Cambridge University Press, 1994.

Chardain, Teilhard de. *The Human Phenomenon*. Brighton: Sussex, 1999.

Johansen, T. K. *Plato's Natural Philosophy*. Cambridge: Cambridge University Press, 2004.

Plato. *Plato's Cosmology: The* Timaeus *of Plato*. Translated by F. M. Cornford. London: Routledge, 1937.

PLATO'S KNOWLEDGE

THE SOCRATES OF PLATO'S dialogue *Theaetetus* considered
the theory that to know something is defined by two requirements:
(1) that the claim at issue be true, and (2) that its putative knower be
able to provide an account for how this is so. Socrates proceeds to
reject this theory by embarking on a course of reasoning marked by
the following exchanges:

> SOCRATES [to THEAETETUS]: [You hold that having] a true
> belief with the addition of an account is knowledge?
> THEAETETUS: Precisely.
> SOCRATES: Can it be, Theaetetus, that, all in a moment, we
> have found out today what so many wise men have grown old in
> seeking and have not found?
> THEAETETUS: I, at any rate, am satisfied with our present
> statement, Socrates.
> SOCRATES: Yes, the statement just in itself may well be
> satisfactory; for how can there ever be knowledge without
> an account and right conception? Yet there is one point in the
> theory as stated that does not find favour with me.
> THEAETETUS: What is that?

SOCRATES: What might be considered its most ingenious feature: it says that the ultimate elements [like the axioms of geometry] are unknowable, whereas whatever is complex [like the geometric theorems] can be known.
THEAETETUS: Is that not right?
SOCRATES: We must find out.[1]

Socrates now proceeds to argue that it cannot be right because if every instance of knowing requires an account—which of course must itself consist of known truth—then nothing whatsoever could ever be known because we would be caught up in an infinite regress.

This sort of reasoning—to the effect that an obviously untenable result follows from a projected thesis—has come to be known as a *reductio ad absurdum*, a "reduction to absurdity." It is an ingenious mode of refutatory reasoning that was common among the philosophers and mathematicians of ancient Greece.

Socrates proceeds to exploit this refutation to argue that it cannot be that all knowledge is "discursive" by being grounded in further knowledge. Rather, there must also be knowledge that is "immediate," being grounded in experience rather than mediated by other, prior knowledge. For if knowledge always had to come from knowledge, and always required substantiating preknowledge, its actual acquisition could never get under way.

A further telling objection to the *Theaetetus* theory of knowing, to the effect that knowledge must always be based on validating reasons, was provided by the English philosopher and logician Bertrand Russell (1872–1970) by counterexamples of the following type. Suppose that X accepts a thesis p that itself has the disjunctive of the format q-or-r. But now let it be that this thesis is true only because q is true (which X does not believe), but that it is accepted by X only because he accepts r (which is actually false). Then of course we cannot properly claim that X knows that p. For the sake of specificity, let it be that X is convinced that Jones is in Korea but only because he (erroneously) believes him to be in South Korea (whereas he is actually in North Korea). Then X's belief is true

---

1. Plato, *Theaetetus*, in *Plato's Theory of Knowledge: The* Theaetetus *and* Sophist *of Plato*, trans. F. M. Cornford (London: Routledge, 1935), 202C–E.

(because Jones indeed is in Korea) and believed by X on the basis of a cogent rationale (namely, his—mistaken—belief that Jones is in South Korea).

The *Theaetetus* theory is thus clearly flawed. Knowledge is more than believed truth, it is *appropriately* believed truth. To count as knowledge a belief must not only be true, its possessor must have an appropriate basis for believing so.

In recent discussion this point has been driven home by a widely cited proposal by the American philosopher Edward Gettier (born 1927).[2] His counterexample is along the lines of the seaman who (correctly) believes that the distant island he is approaching is inhabited, but he believes so only because he mistakes some large shrubs for people. He believes truly and actually has grounds for his belief, but the two are spoilingly disconnected.

The point that emerges from this range of deliberations is that the view that knowledge is true and justified belief is inadequate. For if the considerations that ground the belief in question are out of sync with the facts that ensure the truth of this belief—it no longer makes any sense to speak of knowledge. Knowing is not just a matter of having *some* grounds or reasons for accepting a truth: it requires *appropriate* grounds, and knowledge is not merely belief that is true and justifiably accepted but rather a true belief that is justifiably accepted *as such*.

In implementing the idea of equating knowledge with justified true belief, one cannot and must not treat justification and truth as separate and separable factors. For the correlation will not work if its equivocal stipulation is construed as "believed to be true with *some* justification." It must instead be construed as "believed to be true with *adequate* justification."

For the justification at issue cannot lie merely in the eyes of the knower as a subjective impression; it must obtain objectively in a way that holds not just for the knower but for everyone. The critical distinction between "He merely thinks he knows it" and "He actually does know it" cannot be bypassed. If you permit any separation between justification and truth in that formula, the paradox of

---

2. Edward Gettier, "Is Justified True Belief Knowledge?" *Analysis* 23 (1963): 121–23.

Plato-Russell-Gettier becomes unavoidable. Knowledge is not just a matter of belief that is justified and accepted as true; it is a matter of what is justifiably and correctly accepted as true.

RELATED ANECDOTES

96. Putnam's Twin Earth **268**
99. Searle's Chinese Room **276**

FURTHER READING

Huemer, Michael. *Epistemology: Contemporary Readings.* London: Routledge, 2002.

Moser, P. K., H. Mulder, and J. D. Trout. *The Theory of Knowledge.* Oxford: Oxford University Press, 1998.

Plato. *Theaetetus.* In *Plato's Theory of Knowledge: The Theaetetus and Sophist of Plato,* translated by F. M. Cornford. London: Routledge, 1935.

Runciman, W. *Plato's Later Epistemology.* Cambridge: Cambridge University Press, 1962.

Sosa, Ernest, Jaegwon Kim, and Matthew McGrath, eds. *Epistemology: An Anthology.* 2nd ed. Oxford: Blackwell, 2008.

White, N. P. *Plato on Knowledge and Reality.* Indianapolis: Hackett, 1976.

16

ARISTOTLE'S SEA BATTLE

AS PLATO'S PRIZE PUPIL Aristotle (384–322 BC) saw it, the future is a blank page, awaiting the writing of unfolding history. In line with this view, he wrote as follows in chapter 9 of his study *On Interpretation*:

> A sea-fight must either take place to-morrow or not, but it is not necessary that it should take place to-morrow, neither is it necessary that it should not take place, yet it is necessary that it either should or should not take place to-morrow. Since propositions correspond not with facts, it is evident that then in future events there is a real alternative, and a potentiality in contrary directions, the corresponding affirmation and denial have the same character. . . . One of the two propositions in such instances must be true and the other false, but we cannot say determinately that this or that is false, but must leave the alternative undecided. One may indeed be more likely to be true than the other, but it cannot be either actually true or actually false. It is therefore plain that it is not necessary that for an affirmation and a denial one should be true and the other

false. For in the case of that which exists potentially, but not actually, the rule which applies to that which exists actually does not hold good.[1]

Thus those inimical fleet commanders may or may not choose to engage tomorrow. Only time will tell. Accordingly, Aristotle held that a claim regarding a contingent event in the open fashion has no truth status at present, that is, it is presently neither true nor false.

In regard to the occurrence of that sea battle, the issue is open, undetermined. And so given such a future-appertaining proposition p we must have it then $N(p$ or not-$p)$ but will neither have Np nor $N(\text{not-}p)$, where N indicates necessity. And both p and not-p will accordingly have the same truth-condition, namely, that of indeterminate contingency, of being neither necessarily true, nor not necessarily false.

Such a view of things rejects any predeterministic fatalism. It sees the undecided future as presently open, its development subject to the as-yet uncertain operation of choice and chance. And it sees the contingency of metaphysics as coordinating hand-and-glove with the semantical indeterminacy of logic.

RELATED ANECDOTES

5. Heraclitus's River   **20**
23. St. Augustine's Time   **68**
26. Omar Khayyám's Finger   **79**

FURTHER READING

Whitaker, C. W. A. *Aristotle's De interpretatione: Contradiction and Dialectic.* Oxford: Clarendon, 1996.

---

1. Aristotle, *On Interpretation*, I 9, 19a30–b5.

17

ARISTOTLE'S PRECEPT
ON PRECISION

HOW IS IT THAT we are content with rough forecasts in medicine or meteorology but demand precision in chemistry and physics? Why employ different standards in different areas of deliberation? On this, as on many other key issues in human affairs, Aristotle had some well-developed views. At the outset of his *Nichomachean Ethics* he wrote:

> Precision is not to be sought for alike in all discussions, any more than in all the products of the crafts.... We must be content, then, in speaking of various subjects and with such premises to indicate the truth roughly and in general terms, and in speaking about things which are only for the most part true and with premises of the same kind to reach conclusions that are no better. In the same spirit, therefore, should each type of statement be received; for it is the mark of an educated man *to look for precision in each class of things just so far as the nature of the subject admits*; it is evidently equally foolish to accept probable reasoning from a mathematician and to demand from a rhetorician scientific proofs.[1]

---

1. Aristotle, *Nichomachean Ethics*, trans. W. D. Ross (Oxford: Oxford University Press, 1959), I 3, B12–27; emphasis added.

Few passages in the history of philosophy offer a wiser and more instructive observation than this. And its advice holds good every bit as much in our day as in Aristotle's. For he was surely right in holding that we must have very different expectations in regard to generality, exactness, and precision when it comes to different branches of investigation. Yet things stand rather different as regards his rationale for this view.

Aristotle's reasons were grounded in his views about the nature of natural science, which in their turn were based on the doctrines of his metaphysics. For Aristotle looked in the world's realities from the vantage point of time, maintaining that in describing how things are in nature and how they function we have to distinguish those features that obtain

- timelessly (as with mathematical abstractions)
- always and ever
- generally and for the most part
- sometimes and occasionally
- never ever

Temporal regularity in comportment is the key here,[2] and in those pivotal initial cases we deal with matters that prevail always or for the most part, in contrast with the rest that are merely occasional and sporadic. Now, as Aristotle saw it, the former define the domain of *science*, which addresses what is regularly (though not necessarily invariably) the case.[3] They address the timeless (mathematics), the sempiternal (stellar astronomy), and the generally regular (proximate astronomy and terrestrial physics and certain aspects of the biological and the social realm). Beyond this there is the domain of the merely occasional and intermittent: the realm of the accidental, which falls outside the purview of science. Here we enter the

---

2. On the role of time in Aristotle's conception of science, see Jaakko Hintakka, *Time and Necessity: Studies in Aristotle's Theory of Modality* (Oxford: Clarendon, 1973).

3. On Aristotle's idea of "for the most part qualification of lawful generality," see Gisela Striker, "Notwendigkeit mit Lücken," *Neue Hefte für Philosophie* 24–25 (1985): 146–64. Its role in Aristotle's theory of science is discussed in Lindsay Judson, "Chance and Always or For the Most Part," in *Aristotle's Physics: A Collection of Essays*, ed. Lindsay Judson (Oxford: Clarendon, 1991), 73–99.

realm of chance (*tuchê*) and accident (*symbebetokos*), where scientific explanation is not in prospect. Generality and temporal stability are the pivotal considerations for amenability to science: For Aristotle, the absence or at least infrequency of "accidental" departures from lawful rulishness is the pivot of scientific intelligibility. (In consequence, medicine, for example, is for Aristotle an art rather than a science.)

Viewed from this vantage point, science is a matter of the search for patterns of regularity, and temporal stability thus becomes the key to scientific understanding. And this approach meshes smoothly with Aristotle's view of the metaphysics of existence. For as he saw it, the natural world consists of distinct realms, as follows:

(1) the outer heavens, the sphere of the fixed stars
(2) the inner heavens, the realm of the sun, the planets, and the moon
(3) the Earth in relation to its physical constituents, earth, water, air, and fire
(4) the earth's biological realm in relation to its living occupants, including humans, animals, and plants

Each sphere exhibits regularities that provide a basis for scientific understanding—but this obtains to very different degrees. The fixed stars function with perfect regularity; the inner heavens exhibit more intricate and convoluted patterns of regularity; the realm of earth-correlative material is a halfway house sometimes admitting accidental departures from the general rule of things; while the biological realm is in part regular and in part replete with accidental irregularity and admits of no general (let alone invariable) laws. The more closely earthbound the phenomena, the less amenable they are to strictly scientific understanding, and the more remotely celestial, the more open they are to scientific understanding.

In this light, the contrast between our modern science and that of Aristotle's is instructive. For Aristotle was willing to contemplate a science whose generalizations are just that—generalizations rather than strict universalizations. He was prepared to accept explanatory "laws" that hold "generally and for the most part" rather than insisting in rigid universality. And at the dawn of the scientific enterprise this was not only reasonable but also virtually necessary. For when our inquiries into nature had to be based wholly in the data afforded by the unassisted senses, an empirical science committed to strict universalization would have to go empty-handed in the light of the precision-tenability tradeoff. Science would then have been immobilized at the starting line from which the Greeks began, with the domain of pure mathematics standing by itself in splendid isolation.

And so, while Aristotle and the moderns are on the same page in much of their metascientific thinking, an area of profound disagreement nevertheless remains. For Aristotle exiled the study of human affairs from the sphere of scientific understanding to the status of an art whose conduct was to be guided by a merely practical coping instructed by judgment on the basis of empirical experiences rather than scientific understanding. As he saw it, science is dedicated to generality rather than particularity and to timelessness rather than transiency, whereas the practical arts will address a variable particularity that is concrete and time-bound.

Most moderns, with their commitment to a sizable range of social sciences, take a very different view of the matter. But it is perhaps not totally unfair to say that the jury is yet still out on whether they are correct in this departure from the position of the great Stagirite.

RELATED ANECDOTES

FURTHER READING

Ackrill, J. L. *Aristotle the Philosopher.* Oxford: Oxford University Press, 1981. See especially chap. 7, "The Philosophy of Science."

Aristotle. *Nichomachean Ethics.* Translated by W. D. Ross. Oxford: Oxford University Press, 1959.

Evans, Melbourne G. *The Physical Philosophy of Aristotle.* Albuquerque: University of New Mexico Press, 1964.

18

ARISTOTLE'S GOLDEN MEAN

ARISTOTLE TAUGHT THAT A guiding standard of human "virtue" or excellence is constituted by a proportionate intermediation between opposed extremes of insufficiency and surfeit. As he put it in his *Nicomachean Ethics*:

> [In matters of conduct] as in everything that is continuous and divisible, it is possible to take a lot or a little or a middling amount, the proper amount is something intermediate between excess and insufficiency. [And accordingly] virtue (*arête*) is a mean (*meson*) between two vices, one of excess and one of deficiency, being an intermediary in relation to which the vices respectively fall short or exceed that which is right alike in reaction and in action, while virtue finds and chooses the [appropriate] intermediary (*meson*).[1]

Thus as Aristotle saw it, the "virtue" at issue in humane excellence pivots on getting the right balance between too little and too much.

---

1. Aristotle, *Nicomachean Ethics*, trans. W. D. Ross (Oxford: Oxford University Press, 1959), 1106a26–1107a3.

Table I. Virtue as intermediation

Mode of Comportment	Flawed Insufficiency	Mediating Excellence	Flawed Excess
Self-Projection	Fearfulness/ Cowardice	Courage	Rashness
Care for Assets	Stinginess/ Meanness	Liberality	Profligacy
Self-Treatment	Self-Denial	Temperance	Self-Indulgence
Self-Indulgence	Asceticism	Moderation	Licentiousness
Care for Self-Standing	Self-Centeredness	Proper Self-Regard	Self-Heedlessness
Care for One's Self-Image	Self-Abasement	Self-Respect	Self-Aggrandise-ment
Self-Revelation	Secretiveness	Candor	Blabber-mouthiness
Self-Risk	Over-Caution	Prudence	Foolhardiness
Self-Sharing	Stinginess	Generosity	Profligacy
Self-Involvement	Callous Indifference	Neighborliness	Busibodyness
Self-Esteem	Self-Denigration	Seemly Modesty	Conceit
Self-Interest	Spendthrift	Prudence	Avarice
Self-Assertiveness	Pusillanimity	Righteous Integrity	Irascibility
Verbal Self-Manifestation	Dullness	Ready Wit	Buffoonery

And he substantiated this view on the basis of numerous illustrations along the lines of table I, explaining this doctrine of what Horace was to call a golden mean (*aurea mediocritas*). For example,

the man who fears nothing is foolhardy; the man who fears everything is a pusillanimous coward; however, the man who fears on
rare but appropriate occasions is courageous (1116b15). Neither the
self-denial of asceticism nor the overindulgence of licentiousness
hits the happy medium of a healthy care for the body's requirements
(1118b29).[2] The relativization of these criterial means to a mode of
comportment indicates that this way of acting is something that
is not inherently bad or inherently virtuous. Its quantitative aspect
as well as its quality is pivotal. Accordingly, Aristotle was prepared to grasp that "not every action or reaction admits of a mean.
For some have names that already imply negativity, such as spite,
shamelessness, envy, and in the case of actions, adultery, theft, and
murder."[3]

Aristotle thus viewed virtue or excellence (*arête*) as a prefer-
ential disposition (*hexis prohairetikê*) in favor of the things of the
middle way, with appropriateness always calling for a proper
mean (*mesotês*) that is a suitable intermediary (*meson*) between two
complementarily correlative vices of excess or insufficiency. What
table 2 clearly indicates is that any sort of intermediation has to
proceed *in point of some particular mode of comportment* (here represented by that initial column). And in each case of such Aristotelian
examples, this variable parameter is some reflexive (self-oriented)
mode of personal comportment that ranges over a wide spectrum of degree or intensity. The human virtues or excellences
that stand at the forefront of Aristotle's concerns always involve
some quantitatively comparable feature of self-concern that can be
present with either insufficiency or excess. And proper virtue
lies in realizing this factor to the right and proper extent as between too little and too much along a generally continuous spec-

---

2. Contrary to various interpreters, I propose understanding what is here
    termed "modes of comportment" as types of reaction (*pathê*) generally, and
    not merely or even principally as *emotional* reactions. (For the contrary view,
    see George N. Terzis, "Homeostasis and the Mean in Aristotle's Ethics," in
    Aristotle, Virtue, and the Mean, special issue, *Aperion* 25, no. 4 [December 1995]:
    175–89).

3. Aristotle, *Nicomachean Ethics*, 107a9ff. Compare the *Eudemean Ethics*, 1221b20ff.
    Aristotle might have added that some modes of action are inherently good,
    such as honesty or trustworthiness.

trum.[4] For Aristotle, personal virtue is accordingly determined by a proportion (1107a1) and thereby acquires a decidedly mathematical character.[5]

A striking turn in thought arises here. For us nowadays the crux of ethics is morality, and its object is specifically moral goodness, so that, as we see it, the crux of ethics is acting with due heed for the interests of others. By contrast, Aristotle takes a very different and broader view. For him, ethics is part of a larger triad, according as one's concern is for the condition of people at large (*politikê*), people proximate to oneself (*oikonomia*), and one's own self (*ethikê*). As Aristotle saw it, the object of the ethical enterprise is not the (moral) *goodness of man* but rather the *good for man* more broadly construed to encompass the prime desiderata of justice, health, and affection (1099a26). His ethics aims at achieving a deservedly satisfying life of personal excellence and worth (1099a21), and its target is not a specifically *moral* comportment along the dimension of good and evil but rather proper behavior at large (1094b14). Accordingly, Aristotle's ethical project was something rather different from that of our contemporaries.

Aristotle even found a political application for his ethical doctrine of normative intermediation: "You cannot make a city of ten men, and if there are a hundred thousand it is a city no longer. But the proper number is presumably not a single number, but anything that falls between certain fixed points."[6] Though fixing too small a limit on city size, Aristotle should nevertheless be credited with the important point that in these numerical cases the suitable mean need not be a precise quality but can lie within an indefinite range. Quantitative reasoning is both possible and useful in situations where we cannot be exact about the quantities at issue. One need not know just how much rainfall there will be in order to make it sensible to take one's umbrella.

---

4. Compare with Aristotle, *The Nicomachean Ethics*, trans. H. Joachim (Oxford: Clarendon, 1951), 89–90.

5. W. D. Ross—and many others—render *hôrismenê logô* (at 1107a1) as being determined by a "rational principle," but it could just as well be rendered as "definite ratio" or "fixed proportion"—as the present context invites.

6. Aristotle, *Nicomachean Ethics*, 1170b30–32.

RELATED ANECDOTES

FURTHER READING

Aristotle. *The Nicomachean Ethics.* Translated by W. D. Ross. Oxford: Oxford University Press, 1959.

Joachim, Harold Henry. *Aristotle: The Nicomachean Ethics; A Commentary.* Oxford: Clarendon, 1955.

Pakaluk, Michael. *Aristotle's Nicomachean Ethics: And Introduction.* Cambridge: Cambridge University Press, 2005.

Rescher, Nicholas. *Studies in Quantitative Philosophizing.* Frankfurt: ONTOS, 2010.

Ross, W. D. *Aristotle.* New York: Meridian, 1959.

19

PILATE'S TRUTH

PONTIUS PILATE (CA. 20 BC-50 AD) was the fifth prefect of the Roman province of Judea, serving from 26 to 36 AD, and was famed as the official who authorized the execution of Jesus. St. John's gospel features him in the dialogue: "Pilate thereupon said unto him, Art thou a king then? Jesus answered, Thou sayest that I am a king. To this end I was born, and for this cause came I into the world, that I should bear witness unto the truth. Every one that is of the truth heareth my voice. Pilate saith unto him, *What is truth?* And when he had said this he went out" (John 18:37–38). The episode occasioned the classic line of Francis Bacon's *Essay on Truth*: "What is truth? asked Jesting Pilate; and would not stay for an answer."

The problem of truth has been a key focus of philosophical deliberation since Plato's day. The salient questions are, (1) What is truth: just what is it that must be the case when a thesis is said to be true; what is contained in a truth-claim? (2) How is this condition to be determined: what sorts of evidential indications justify us in attributing truth to a thesis; what sorts of preconditions can warrant a truth-claim? And the problem is that these two factors may not be in perfect alignment: that there can be an information gap between warrant and content. (We readily acknowledge all sorts of individuals as truly fellow humans, without, for example, predetermining the essential requisite that their parents, of whom we may well know nothing, were also human.)

To be sure, the conception of truth is such that a claim p qualifies as true when (and only when) what it affirms is actually the case: it is a fact. (Truth, as the medievals said, is *adaequatio ad rem*.) But this is of little help because we have no cognitive access to the facts apart from what we *think* to be the case and thereby accept as true.

RELATED ANECDOTES

FURTHER READING

Kirkham, Richard L. *Theories of Truth: A Critical Introduction.* Cambridge: MIT Press, 1992.

Moser, P. K., H. Mulder, and J. D. Trout. *The Theory of Knowledge.* Oxford: Oxford University Press, 1998.

Sosa, Ernest, Jaegwon Kim, and Matthew McGrath, eds. *Epistemology: An Anthology.* Oxford: Blackwell, 2008.

20

ARCHIMEDES'S LEVER

THE GREEK MATHEMATICIAN, PHYSICIST, and astron-
omer Archimedes (287–212 BC) is famously reported as saying,
"Give me a place to stand, and [with a lever] I will move the
whole world [*Dos moi pou sto kai kino teal gael*]."[1] Reacting to this
claim, Mark Twain joked as follows:

> "Give me whereon to stand," said Archimedes, "and I will move
> the earth." The boast was a pretty safe one, for Archimedes
> knew quite well that the standing place was wanting, and
> always would be wanting. But suppose he had moved the
> earth, what then? What benefit would it have been to anybody?
> The job would never have paid working expenses, let alone
> dividends, and so what was the use of talking about it? From
> what astronomers tell us, I should reckon that the earth moved
> quite fast enough already, and if there happened to be a few
> cranks who were dissatisfied with its rate of progress, as far

1. The prime source is Simplicius, *On Aristotle's Physics*, found in C. A. Brandis,
   ed., *Handbuch der Geschichte der Griechisch-romischen Philosophie* (Berlin, 1835),
   424a.

as I am concerned, they might push it along for themselves; I would not move a finger or subscribe a penny piece to assist in anything of the kind.[2]

Of course Twain was right. No one was going to give Archimedes that firm, moveable place for his lever. The experiment he envisioned was feasible only in thought. But such thought experimentation has always been prominent in science and philosophy alike. What are Xenophanes's animal theologians or Buridan's ass but thought experiments?

An important philosophical idea lies at the root of Archimedes's contention—one that was to become known as the principle of the uniformity of nature.

After all, levers work when we shift stories or pry lids open, so why not as an astronomical side? And when we study mechanisms and chemistry and bridges here on Earth among the local recourses and conditions that prevail in our terrestrial domain we do not hesitate to claim universal applicability for the generalizations we find and boldly call them "laws of nature."

We often base conclusions on thought experiments as readily as open actual ones. The problem of the rational justification of this audacious proceeding is something that has long preoccupied philosophers and remains subject to contention down to the present day.

RELATED ANECDOTES

FURTHER READING

Horowitz, Tamara, and Gerald Massey, eds. *Thought Experiments in Science and Philosophy*. Savage: Rowman and Littlefield, 1991.

Rescher, Nicholas. *What If: Thought Experimentation in Philosophy*. New Brunswick: Transaction, 2005.

Sorenson, Roy A. *Thought Experiments*. Oxford: Oxford University Press, 1992.

---

2. "Archimedes," *Australian Standard*, 1887; first published under the pseudonym Twark Main.

21

THE SHIP OF THESEUS

IN HIS STORY OF the ship of Theseus, the Greek historian and moralist Plutarch (ca. 48–125 AD) propounded a puzzle that soon split philosophers into rival schools:

> The ship wherein *Theseus* and his young Athenians returned from *Crete* had thirty oars, and was preserved by the Athenians down even to the time of Demetrius Phalereus, for they took away the old planks as they decayed, putting in new and stronger timber in their place, in so much that this rebuilt ship became a standing example among the philosophers, for the logical question of the identity of things; one side holding that the ship remained the same, and the other contending that it was not the same.[1]

Much the same issue was posed by Thomas Hobbes's example of Sir John Cutler's stockings, which in the course of time wore out totally, bit by bit, with every hole repaired by darning needle and

---

1. Plutarch, *Life of Theseus*, in *Plutarch's Lives of Illustrious Men*, ed. A. H. Clough, trans. John Dryden (Boston: Little, Brown and Company, 1880), 7–8.

a thread until ultimately nothing of the original material recurred. Was the ultimate result still the same pair of stockings?

So with regard to physical objects like boats and stockings, just what is it that determines transtemporal sameness or identity? Is it material continuity, with structure playing a secondary (or even nonexistent) role, or is it structural continuity, with materials playing a secondary (or even nonexistent) role? Is it process or product that is paramount? And is the whole issue one of nature or of mere convention?

And what of immaterial objects? When you play a piece on the piano and then the violin is it still "the same piece"? And if you translate a Homeric epic from Greek into English, is it still the same work? Such puzzles tend to divide people into different schools. But what does this mean for the philosophical enterprise?

The theorists of a "positivistic" orientation would say that the issue is pointless because such questions have no tenable answer at all. Their "doctrinalistic" opponents would counter that there is just one right answer: majority rules—as long as most of the original material remains, that boat or stocking is the same, but after that it becomes different. And the "contextualist" would say that it all depends on the purposive context in the Theseus case, as long as the same groups of seamen are involved in a common voyage in that slow changing craft—that is, as long as the vessel's role in the story exhibits such continuity, it remains the same boat.

So what we have here is a typical philosophical debate where different "schools of thought" arise to advocate different and discordant resolutions.

The explanation for such sharp differences of philosophical opinion is not far to seek. After all, the task of the subject is to engage with fundamental and far-ranging questions regarding the relation of ourselves to our fellows and to the world we share in common. Addressing these matters unavoidably involves basic issues of outlook and orientation. For if you function in the evidentiary context of a historian, there is no question but that you are bound to see the ship as the same; while for the issue of maritime insurance, it could well fail to count as such. So it is more than likely that when we disagree regarding "the same X"—the same person, or poem, or ship—what is actually at issue may well not be a single universal idea but a variety of distinct matters differentiated by purposive considerations.

RELATED ANECDOTES

FURTHER READING

Chisholm, R. M. *Person and Object*. Chicago: Open Court, 1976.
Plutarch. *Life of Theseus*. In *Plutarch's Lives of Illustrious Men*. Edited by A. H. Clough. Translated by John Dryden. Boston: Little, Brown and Company, 1880.

22

TERTULLIAN'S ABSURDITY

QUINTUS SEPTIMUS TERTULLIAN(US) (ca. 160–ca. 225 AD) was a prolific Christian theologian from Carthage in the Roman province of Africa. Counted among the founding fathers of Catholic theology, he wrote both technical philosophical explanations of Christian doctrines and apologetic polemics in their defense. He inaugurated its Trinitarian creedal expression of God as being "Three in person but one in substance." In one of his Christological works, Tertullian wrote "And buried, He rose again: it is certain, because impossible [*Et sepultus resurrexit; certum est, quia impossibile*]."[1] On the basis of this statement Tertullian has been (mis)credited throughout the ages with the dictum: "I believe it because it is absurd [*Credo quia absurdum*]." While the "it" at issue was unquestionably the Resurrection, it has often been (mis)taken to be the Trinity because of Tertullian's linkage to this doctrine.

It seems to have been Tertullian's view that the teaching in questions is so extraordinary that people would never have accepted

---

1. Tertullian, *De carne Christi*, ed. and trans. Earnest Evans (London: SPCK, 1956), chap. 5, 4.

it in the absence of very strong and convincing grounds for doing so. The idea that in theological matters absurdity betokens credibility has stimulated much interest.

Tertullian's deliberations set afoot an ever-continuing controversy regarding the disconnection between the "higher" claims and truths of religion and the lesser garden-variety claims and truths of everyday life—let alone those of theoretical science. Ironically, a Trinitarian prospect looms here: Are we dealing with something that is one in essence (actual truth) but of three distinct types: religious, scientific, and commonplace? Philosophers throughout the ages have debated the question of the constitution of these categories, and the possibility of an inconsistency here has always entranced them. The Catholic Church's steadfast insistence on their compatibility should, by rights, have earned it much credit.

RELATED ANECDOTES

3. Xenophanes's Animal Theologians   15
21. The Ship of Theseus   63
30. Averroes's Truth   88

FURTHER READING

Barnes, T. D. *Tertullian: A Literary and Historical Study.* Oxford: Clarendon, 1971; revised ed. 1985.
Kelly, J. N. D. *Early Christian Doctrines.* New York: Harper, 1958.

23

ST. AUGUSTINE'S TIME

SPACE AND TIME HAVE preoccupied philosophers from their subject's very start, but they found the former—time—to be something that is especially baffling because virtually the whole of it just does not exist at present—or indeed ever, at any particular juncture. Thus St. Augustine of Hippo (354–430) wrote:

> For what is time? Who can easily and briefly explain it? Who even in thought can comprehend it, even to the pronouncing of a word concerning it? But what in speaking do we refer to more familiarly and knowingly than time? And certainly we understand when we speak of it; we understand also when we hear it spoken of by another. What, then, is time? If no one asks of me, I know; if I wish to explain to him who asks, I know not. Yet I say with confidence, that I know that if nothing passed away, there would not be past time; and if nothing were coming, there would not be future time; and if nothing were, there would not be present time. Those two times, therefore, past and future, how are they, when even the past now is not; and the future is not as yet? But should the present be always present, and should it not pass into time past, time truly it could not be, but eternity.

> If, then, time present—if it be time—only comes into existence
> because it passes into time past, how do we say that even this is,
> whose cause of being is that it shall not be—namely, so that we
> cannot truly say that time is, unless because it tends not to be?[1]

All this seems very puzzling. If the future does not now exist,
when will it come to be? All we can offer is the (effectively circular) response "in the future," which certainly seems to be begging
the question. (And the past is in essentially the same boat—for just
where is it now? Answer: "in the past.")

To all appearances, the present alone is currently real, with the
past long gone and the future not available. Perhaps time is only in
the mind, an illusion of sorts inherent in how our thought wanders
over what is in fact a vast but unchanging landscape. From Parmenides in antiquity through Kant to F. H. Bradley in the twentieth century, various philosophers have thought something like that,
and even some contemporary physicists hold analogous views. But
even if time is rooted in thought, does that not itself presuppose the
reality of time since thought is ever changing? Perhaps time is only
a matter of mere appearances, but systemically stable appearances
themselves constitute a reality of sorts. And in the end we cannot
manage to think coherently about things without reference to time.
For when we make such claims as "It is raining" or "I am hungry,"
time becomes the crucial factor in the determination of truth and
falsity and thereby an essential factor in meaningful communication.

It is regrettable that there is no fully satisfactory way of explaining what is at issue here. For time apparently is one of those elemen-
tal realities that just has to be understood on its own terms, being
"unanalyzable," as logicians incline to say. Much though we would
like to combine space and time (and wish for the "space-time" unifi-
cation of which relativity theory speaks), the fact remains that those
two potencies play very different roles in our lives, and to speak of
"time travel" is to amalgamate very different things and claim for
the one what belongs to the other.

---

1. St. Augustine, *The Confessions of St. Augustine*, trans. E. B. Pusey (London: T.
Nelson and Sons, 1937), book 11, chap. 14, para. 17.

But baffling though time is in its resistance to descriptive characterization by means of the stabilities of language, it is a pervasive and crucially important factor in our life and our thought. For we cannot escape the daunting realization that we ourselves and pretty well everything about us are "here today, gone tomorrow." For us, time is a framework within which—inevitably—we live and move and have our being. We may, just possibly, be able to think it away. But even then, there yet remains the realization that reality is impervious to what we think about it.

RELATED ANECDOTES

FURTHER READING

Augustine. *The Confessions of St. Augustine.* Translated by E. B. Pusey. London: T. Nelson and Sons, 1937.

Bardon, Adrian. *A Brief History of the Philosophy of Time.* Oxford: Oxford University Press, 2013.

Gale, Richard M., ed. *The Philosophy of Time.* London: Palgrave-Macmillan, 1968.

Hawking, Stephen. *A Brief History of Time.* New York: Bantam, 1988.

PART

2

THE MIDDLE AGES,
500–1500

24

AVICENNA'S PLANK

MAN, *HOMO SAPIENS*, IS an amphibian who lives in a world of nature but also in a world of thought. And the two aspects can readily fall out of step, with thought coming to be at odds with the reality of things. In particular, many is the time we exaggerate the magnitude of the obstacles that confront us.

The Persian philosopher Avicenna (980–1037) projected in his encyclopedic treatise *Kitâb al-shifâ* a story that ran roughly as follows: "A man was challenged to cross a deep chasm on a solid wooden plank fixed securely on the opposite side. He balked at the very idea and flatly declined the challenge. But when exactly the same plank was laid out on the ground, he crossed it cheerfully with bounding steps."[1]

The difference of course lies in the imagination's contemplation of (often remote) possibilities. With that plank, it is less the actualities of the situation that are so different in the two cases and more so

---

1. For this example, see Fazlur Rahman's translation in *Avicenna's De Anima: Being the Psychological Part of the Kitâb al-shifâ* (Oxford: Oxford University Press, 1959).

the possibilities. What is fundamentally one and the same challenge will grow increasingly ominous as the penalty of a possible failure increases and we confront some daunting "what if" prospect.

Yet why should there be this dramatic difference here? Objectively considered, the task at issue with this transit is of course no more difficult in the one case than in the other. But in the end it is always our subjective reality—reality as we see it—with which we must deal in our decisions regarding matters of action. Our only road to what is proceeds via what we think to be.

RELATED ANECDOTES

FURTHER READING

James, William. *Principles of Psychology.* New York: Henry Holt, 1890.

Rahman, Fazlur, ed. *Avicenna's De Anima: Being the Psychological Part of Kitâb al-shifâ.* Oxford: Oxford University Press, 1959.

25

BURIDAN'S ASS

CAN A REASONABLE AGENT choose a course of action or select an object in the absence of any preference? It certainly appears on first view that this question must be answered negatively. For by the very concept of a "reasonable agent," it is requisite that such an individual have *reasons* for their actions. And when a reasonable choice among alternatives is made, this must, it would seem, have to be based upon a *preference* for the object actually chosen vis-à-vis its available alternatives. Where there is no *preference*, it would appear that no *reason* for a selection can exist, so that there apparently cannot be a *reasonable* way of making a choice. This line of reasoning seems to establish the precept: *No reasonable choice without a preference.*

However, despite the surface plausibility of this argument, it cannot be accepted as fully correct. For there is a well-known, indeed notorious, counterexample: the dilemma or paradox of Buridan's ass, named after the French schoolman Jean Buridan (ca. 1300–ca. 1360). This hypothetical animal is hungry and positioned midway between essentially identical bundles of hay. There is assumed to be no reason why the animal should have a preference for one of the bundles of hay over the other. Yet it must eat one or the other of them or else starve. Under these circumstances, the creature will, being reasonable, prefer having-one-bundle-of-hay to having-no-bundle-of-hay. It therefore *must choose one* of the bundles. Yet there are, by hypothesis, simply no *reasons* for preferring either bundle. It appears to follow that reasonable choice must—somehow—be possible in the absence of preference.[1]

The issue of indifferent choice fits in a very natural and congenial way into the problem context of Buridan's theory of the will. The will, he holds, does not decide spontaneously from within its own resources, but it is subject to the commands of reason. As reason judges, so rules the will. When reason deems one object a greater good than another, the will can only opt—other things being equal—for the greater good. Should reason deem two of its objects wholly equivalent, the will would be unable to act by breaking the deadlock of itself. Buridan supports this intellectual determinism of the will by saying that those who claim free will for man but deny it to animals find themselves in difficult straits: "It seems to me that, to show the difference between the freedom of our will and the lack of freedom to which the actuating faculty of a dog is subject, it would be better to trust to faith than to natural reason. For it would be difficult indeed to show that when our will is wholly indifferent between two opposed acts, it [in contradistinction to the actuating faculty of a dog] could decide for one or the

---

1.   Buridan's ass does not occur in his extant writings. There is no question, however, but that Buridan was familiar, in essence, with the example to which he lent his name. In his unpublished commentary on Aristotle's *De Caelo*, in a gloss on section 2, 13, Buridan gives the example of a dog—not an ass!—dying of hunger between two equal portions of food. See L. Minio-Paluello's article "Buridan" in the *Encyclopedia Britannica* (1956 edition). This almost, though not quite, bears out Schopenhauer's conjecture that Buridan's example was adopted from that of Aristotle's man perplexed by a choice between food and drink but that Buridan "changed the man to an ass, solely because it was the custom of this parsimonious Scholastic to take for his example either Socrates and Plato, or *asinum*" (Schopenhauer, *Prize Essay on the Freedom of the Will* [Cambridge: Cambridge University Press, 2006], 59). It would clearly be unseemly to present the greats in perplexity.

other alternative without being so determined by some external factor."[2] It is therefore easy to see how, in the context of Buridan's theory of will, the ass example might, with its characteristic double-edgedness, serve either (1) as a somewhat drastic example in illustration of Buridan's intellectual determinism of the will or (2) as an example adduced by Buridan's opponents in an attempt to render this doctrine absurd.

It deserves stress that the non-preferential choice problem serves also to highlight the difference between *reasons* and *motives*. When a random selection among indifferent objects is made by me, I do have a *reason* for my particular selection, namely, the fact that it was indicated to me by a random selector. But I have no *preference* or psychological motivation of other sorts to incline me to choose this item instead of its (by hypothesis indifferent) alternatives. Such absence of a psychologically motivating preference does not, however, entail the impossibility of a logically justifiable selection. A choice can, therefore, be logically vindicated as having been made reasonably even though it cannot be traced back to a rationale of differentiating evaluation. In short, we can have *reasons* for a choice even where there is no rational *motive*.

It is an interesting consideration that the problem cannot be resolved by delegating an indifferent choice to a mechanism such as a coin toss or the roll of a die. For consider choosing between *A* and *B* by giving *A* "heads" and *B* "tails." But now there is the entirely indifferent alternative of giving *A* "tails" and *B* "heads." By bringing the die into it we simply re-create the very problem at hand through yet another situation of indifferent choice.

RELATED ANECDOTES

---

2. Jean Buridan, *In Metaphysicam Aristotelis Quaestiones*, quoted by P. Duhem, *Études sur Léonard de Vinci* (Paris: Librairie scientifique A. Hermann et Fils, 1906), 3: 20–21. Duhem in this work attributes these *Quaestiones* on the *Metaphysics* to *another* John Buridan, but in the face of manuscript evidence discovered by himself, he subsequently revised himself (Duhem, *Le Système du Monde* [Paris: A. Hermann, 1917], 4: 126).

FURTHER READING

Copleston, F. C. *A History of Medieval Philosophy*. London: Metheun, 1972.

Rescher, Nicholas. "Choice without Preference: The Problem of 'Buridan's Ass.'" In *Essays in the History of Philosophy*, 77–114. Aldershot: Avebury, 1995.

Zupko, Jack. *John Buridan*. Notre Dame: University of Notre Dame Press, 2003.

26

OMAR KHAYYÁM'S FINGER

A FAMOUS QUATRAIN FROM the *Rubáiyát* of the Persian poet and polymath Omar Khayyám (1048–1131) reads as follows:

> The Moving Finger writes; and, having writ,
> Moves on: not all thy Piety nor Wit
> Shall lure it back to cancel half a Line,
> Nor all thy Tears wash out a word of it.[1]

The underlying fatalism of this Muslim sage not only sees the past as beyond change but the future as well: whatever is to be is written in the book of fate. This view is vividly encapsulated in the classic story of "The Appointment in Samarra," which, in W. Somerset Maugham's retelling, reads as follows:

> There was a merchant in Bagdad who sent his servant to market to buy provisions and in a little while the servant came back, white and trembling, and said, Master, just now when I was in the marketplace I was jostled by a woman in the crowd and when I turned I saw it was Death that jostled me. She looked at me

---

1. Omar Khayyám, *The Rubai'yát of Omar Khayyam*, trans. Edward Fitzgerald (New York: Penguin, 1995).

and made a threatening gesture, now, lend me your horse, and I will ride away from this city and avoid my fate. I will go to Samarra and there Death will not find me. The merchant lent him his horse, and the servant mounted it, and he dug his spurs in its flanks and as fast as the horse could gallop he went. Then the merchant went down to the marketplace and he saw me standing in the crowd and he came to me and said, Why did you make a threating gesture to my servant when you saw him this morning? That was not a threatening gesture, I said, it was only a start of surprise. I was astonished to see him in Bagdad, for I had an appointment with him tonight in Samarra.[2]

The speaker here is Death and the story's most obvious lesson is our human inability to escape its fated embrace. For beyond mortality there is also the further idea of a broader fatalism: destiny has a grand plan for us whose inevitable decrees we can neither avert nor alter.

To be sure this would not mean that we must give up on our efforts to deliberate, to decide, to plan, to worry about what to do. We could not do so, for these activities are part of our nature as humans and our doing these things itself is also part of fate's great plan. So in the end the fact remains that we do—and perhaps must—think that we are in charge.

This fatalistic perspective has been prominent in Western culture and has figured prominently in such religions as Zoroastrianism and Manichaeism. The vigorous opposition to these creeds by Augustine and the other Church Fathers succeeded in most of the Mediterranean world before the rise of Islam entered the contest.

RELATED ANECDOTES

34. Dr. Faustus's Bargain   103
65. William James's Freedom   186

FURTHER READING

Cahn, S. M. *Fate and Logic and Time*. New Haven: Yale University Press, 1967.
Khayyám, Omar. *The Rubai'yât of Omar Khayyam*. Translated by Edward Fitzgerald. New York: Penguin, 1995.
O'Hara, John. *Appointment in Samarra*. New York: Harcourt Brace, 1934.

---

2.   The story is retold in W. Somerset Maugham's 1933 play *Sheppey*.

27

KING ALFONSO'S BOAST

KING ALFONZO X (1221-1284), called "The Learned" (El Sabio), who ruled Castile (and much else) in the middle of the thirteenth century, was a scholar at heart. And upon studying the Ptolemaic system of astronomy with its profusion of cycles and epicycles, he remarked: "If the Lord Almighty had consulted me before embarking on his creation, I would have recommended something simpler."[1]

In this regard, however, the way forward is not as easy as it may seem. For what most fundamentally stands in the way of any conjectural improvability is the all-pervasive interconnection of things.

Suppose that we make only a very small alteration in the descriptive composition of the real, say by adding one pebble to the river bank. But which pebble? Where are we to get it and what are we to put in its place? And where are we to put the air or the water that this new pebble displaces? And when we put that material in a new spot, just how are we to readjust its history as it was? Moreover, the region within six inches of the new pebble used to hold N peb-

---

1. On Alfonso's scholarship, see Robert Burns, *Emperor of Letters* (Philadelphia: University of Pennsylvania Press, 1990).

bles. It now holds $N + 1$. Of which region are we to say that it gave up a pebble and now holds $N - 1$? If it is that region yonder, then how did the pebble get here from there? By a miraculous instantaneous transport? By a little boy picking it up and throwing it. But then, which little boy? And how did he get there? And if he threw it, then what happened to the air that his throw displaced, which would otherwise have gone undisturbed? And as we conjure with those pebbles, what about the structure of the envisioning electromagnetic, thermal, and gravitational fields? Just how are these to be preserved as was, given the removal and/or shift of the pebbles? How is matter to be readjusted to preserve consistency here? Or are we to do so by changing the fundamental laws of physics? Any assumptive change on the real order of things gives rise to further problems without end.

And this means that there is no real prospect of local tinkering with the world without wider ramifications. In this *world*—and indeed in any possible world—states of affairs are so interconnected that local changes always have pervasive consequences. A change at any point has reverberations everywhere. Once you embark on a reality-modifying assumption, then as far as pure logic is concerned all bets are off. Any local "fix" always has involvements throughout, and in consequence no tweaking or tinkering may be able to effect an improvement. For the introduction of belief-contravening hypotheses puts everything at risk. In their wake, nothing is safe anymore. To maintain consistency one must revamp the entire fabric of fact and so confront a task of Sisyphean proportions. Reality is something too complex to be remade more than fragmentally by our thought, which can effectively come to terms only with piecemeal changes *in* reality but not with comprehensive changes *of* reality. Reality's reach has a grip that it will never entirely relax: it is a tight-woven web where the cutting of any thread leads to an unraveling of the whole.

The world we have—and indeed any possible alternative to it—is a package deal. Once we start tinkering with it, it slips away like water between our fingers. In seeking to change it, we create conditions where there is no longer any anaphoric "it" to deal with. To modify so complexly an interlaced system as a "world" is to abolish it—to replace it by something else. And this might well be something that is far, far worse.

Granted, the world's *particular* existing negativities are indeed remediable in theory. But to arrange for this will likely entail an even larger array of negativities overall. The thesis here is effectively that of Leibniz: it is not intended to claim that the world is *perfect*, but just that it is *optimal*—the best possible with the emphasis not on *best* but on *possible*.

Considerations along these lines render the idea that the world's defects can be fixed by hypothetical tinkering is decidedly implausible. And given the fact that revising the world-as-a-whole lies beyond our feeble powers, we have to face up to the consideration that—for all we can tell—this is indeed the best of possible worlds, and that changing the existing condition of the universe in any way whatsoever will diminish the sum total of its positivities. We have to face the prospect that there is no "quick fix" for the negativities of this world. As concerns merit, the existing situation could well be the best overall arrangement of things—its manifest defects to the contrary notwithstanding.

RELATED ANECDOTES

FURTHER READING

Burns, Robert. *Emperor of Letters: Alfonso X.* Philadelphia: University of Pennsylvania Press, 1990.

Gillispie, Charles C., ed. *Dictionary of Scientific Biography.* vol. 1. New York: Scribners, 1970. See the article "Alfonso el Sabio."

Jacobs, W. W. "The Monkey's Paw." In *The Lady of the Barge.* London: Harcourt Brace, 1902.

Leibniz, G. W. *Theodicy: Essays on the Goodness of God, the Freedom of Man, and the Origin of Evil.* Translated by E. M. Huggard. London: Routledge, 1951.

28

SCHOLASTICISM'S OMNIPOTENCE PERPLEX

THE SCHOOLMEN OF THE Middle Ages, who loved theoretical puzzles, confronted a really big one with regard to theistic theology. It was posed by the following line of thought: "God is omnipotent: his power is unlimited—he can do literally anything. But if God can do *anything* at all, then he can set limits to his powers, and perhaps even resign and forgo them altogether. Conceivably he could even annihilate himself—or turn himself into a frog."[1] This sort of thing is clearly inappropriate, and yet it's baffling.

The cleverest among the Scholastics—Thomas Aquinas (1224–1274) for one—had an answer to this dilemma, predicated on taking a closer second look at the very idea of omnipotence. Omnipotence, so they held, does not call for the capacity to do *anything whatever* but rather consists in the capacity to do *anything that it is logically possible to do.* Thus it would not lie in the range of an omnipotent God to reduplicate himself, to turn himself into a mindless creature, to resign his role, or of course, to annihilate himself. Such things are simply impossible.

---

1. The medievals called puzzles of this sort "insolubles" (*insolubilia*). They favored the analysis of such matters because of its role in evoking clarifications.

And the Schoolmen also extended this line of thought to other divine attributes such as omnibenevolence and omniscience. Evil actions are inherently impossible for God. And there are comparable logical restrictions on the knowledge of an omniscient being: He cannot know that which is false (as opposed to knowing of its falsity). Nor yet if the details of an open future are inherently unknowable can it be asked of an omniscient being to know them.

Thus two factors come to the forefront of deliberation here. The first is the question of the nature of things, of what is essential to being an item of a certain kind—a god, for example. For if some feature is definitive of a something as the very thing that it is, then one cannot meaningfully attribute to it some further feature that is incompatible therewith. The analysis of concepts thus becomes a critical issue—a fact that the Schoolmen devoted much effort in this direction.

The second problematic factor relates to the issue of logical possibility. Logic—the study of rational coherence—has to be the arbiter of possibility, and what is involved in logical coherence and what is needed for its realization become pivotal questions. The Schoolmen did not split logical hairs for mere amusement. They had critically important work for logic to do.

RELATED ANECDOTE

26. Omar Khayyám's Finger   **79**

FURTHER READING

Aquinas, Thomas. *Summa Theologica: Questions on God.* Edited by Brian Davies and Brian Leflow. Cambridge: Cambridge University Press, 2006.

Copleston, Frederick C. *Aquinas.* London: Pelican, 1955.

Copleston, Frederick C. *A History of Medieval Philosophy.* New York: Harper and Row, 1972.

Henry, Desmond Paul. *Medieval Logic and Metaphysics: A Modern Introduction.* London: Hutchinson, 1972.

Spade, Paul V. *Lies, Language, and Logic in the Later Middle Ages.* London: Varicorum, 1988.

29

AQUINAS'S PROOFS

IN HIS MAGISTERIAL *SUMMA THEOLOGIAE* the great Italian philosopher and theologian St. Thomas Aquinas (1225–1274) considered a series of "proofs" of the existence of God that have become known as the "Five Ways" (*Quinque viæ*). Like his master Aristotle before him, Aquinas viewed Euclid's *Elements* as the very model of demonstrative reasoning. Cogent demonstration so regarded is a matter of logical deduction from self-evidently obvious premises.

What this meant in the present case is that the argumentation will take some such line as maintaining:

- That God, now by definition seen as the perfect (supreme) being, could not fail to exist since failure here thus would preclude what is (ex hypothesi) his being perfect (supreme).
- That God, now by definition seen as the first and ultimate cause of things, could not fail to exist because in the absence of a finite and ultimate cause nothing whatsoever would exist.

The pivot of Aquinas's five proofs was in each case some pivotal factor of Aristotelian philosophy. And the tenor of the whole discussion is an Aristotelianization of Christian theology as developed by the Church Fathers. As here conceived, Aquinas's God is in effect "the God of the philosophers," a factor in rational systematization rather than a fitting addressee for prayer, devotion, and moral affectionate obedience. But the problem here—troubling to philosophical theologians throughout the years—is the all too evident disconnection between the "metaphysically" abstract conception of God that is at issue in such argumentation as "supreme being" or "ultimate cause" and the Bible's paternalistic conception of God. It is hard to see this metaphysically conceived entity as a caring parent and protector—a concerned, benevolent, and generous being accessible in devotion and prayer with heartfelt care even for each little sparrow.

Granted, there is no reason why the God of the theoreticians and the God of the ordinary believer could not in the end turn out to be one and the same being. But it remains perplexingly mysterious how one and the same being is at issue behind these very different conceptions. And just this is perhaps why Aquinas himself in the end looked to the tradition of Christian rejection to reconcile this duality of a God who addresses both the mind of philosophers and the heart of believers.

RELATED ANECDOTES

14. Plato's Demiurge   41
22. Tertullian's Absurdity   66
28. Scholasticism's Omnipotence Perplex   84
71. Frege's Morning Star   202

FURTHER READING

Aquinas, Thomas. *Summa Theologica: Questions on God.* Edited by Brian Davies and Brian Leflow. Cambridge: Cambridge University Press, 2006.
Maurer, Armand. *Medieval Philosophy.* 2nd ed. Toronto: Pontifical Institute of Medieval Studies, 1982.
Stump, Eleonore. *Aquinas.* London: Routledge, 2003.

30

AVERROES'S TRUTH

THE HISPANO-MUSLIM PHILOSOPHER AVERROES (1226–1298) has the distinction of being credited with a philosophical theory he did not actually hold. The doctrine of Averroism—so called by its opponents—was reputed as a theory of double truth. For it supposedly maintained that "there are two distinct and discordant bodies of truth: that of religion (with its Old Testament doctrine of a world created in time) and that of a science (with its Aristotelian doctrine of any world)."[1] Like the doctrine of solipsism, to the effect that all that actually exists is oneself and one's ideas about things, this too is a doctrine that no one ever actually held in the harsh, unqualified form of its flat-out articulation.

The problem of Averroism in its traditional (albeit misunderstood) format lies in its conflict with the unity of reason. For as Aristotle already insisted, once we deem both p and not-p to be acceptable truths, there is nothing we can coherently say on the

---

1. On this characterization of Averroism, see Etienne Gilson, *History of Philosophy in the Middle Ages* (New York: Random House. 1955).

matter: it has effectively vanished from the landscape of meaningful communication. Granted we can save matters by contextualizing our claims, *p* holds true on Wednesdays and Thursdays and not-*p* during the rest of the week, or again that *p* holds true on one side of the Alps and not-*p* on the other.

What Averroes actually taught is that there is only one authentic truth, but thanks to limitation of the human intellect there indeed are two different ways of apprehending and teaching it. On this perspective, the problem lies not in an indecisive reality but in an ambivalent vacillation of imperfect human thinking. And the Christian Scholastic Siger of Brabant (ca. 1248–1284) took this idea further to contemplate an inherent duality in the human intellect moving on the one side to hard (scientific or philosophical) thinking. He was then accused of the "Averroism" of holding a dual truth theory, with religious truth in flat-out contradiction with the truth of philosophy and reason. This duality was then countered by the Christian saint and philosopher Thomas Aquinas (1224–1274), who, in his tract "On the Unity of the Intellect: Against the Averroists" (*De unitate intellectum contra Averroistas*), argued against any such conflict of truths and upheld the Christian doctrine of the createdness of the world as uniquely correct.

The Averroist position of a dualism of understanding is reflected in the influential contrast drawn by William James between the tender- and tough-minded.

> For every sort of permutation and combination is possible in human nature; and if I now proceed to define more fully what I have in mind when I speak of rationalists and empiricists, by adding to each of those titles some secondary qualifying characteristics, I beg you to regard my conduct as to a certain extent arbitrary. [But in general] rationalism is always monistic. It starts from wholes and universals, and makes much of the unity of things. Empiricism starts from the parts, and makes of the whole a collection—is not averse therefore to calling itself pluralistic. . . . The rationalist finally will be of dogmatic temper in his affirmations, while the empiricist may be more sceptical and open to discussion.

I will write these traits down in two columns. I think you will practically recognize the two types of mental make-up that I mean if I head the columns by the titles 'tender-minded' and 'tough-minded' respectively.

The Tender-Minded	The Tough-Minded
Rationalistic	Empiricist
(going by 'principles'),	(going by 'facts'),
Intellectualistic,	Sensationalistic,
Idealistic,	Materialistic,
Optimistic,	Pessimistic,
Theistic,	Atheistic,
Voluntaristic (free-willist),	Fatalistic,
Monistic,	Pluralistic,
Dogmatical.	Sceptical.[2]

Moreover, the Averroist perspective finds some ultimate justification in modern views about brain lateralization, with the left side prominent for formal (mathematical, logical, "analytic") thinking and the right side for creative (humanistic, emotional, "synthetic") thinking. On this approach too there is a dualization in the approach to "the truth" of things.

It must be stressed, however, that nowadays the theorists of Averroist leanings generally contemplate the prospect of different perceptive perspectives upon a single self-consistent reality. Outright inconsistency is nowadays unpopular among metaphysicians. Only logicians with their interest in "pushing the limits" to determine the boundaries of meaningful discourse have tried to make sense of inconsistent discourse.[3]

RELATED ANECDOTES

---

2. William James, *Pragmatism: The Works of William James* (Cambridge: Harvard University Press, 1975), 12–13.

3. On this theme, see N. Rescher and R. Brandom, *The Logic of Inconsistency* (Oxford: Blackwell, 1976), for an attempt to retain rational coherence and inconsistent commitments.

FURTHER READING

Dodd, Tony. *The Life and Thought of Siger of Brabant*. Lewiston: E. Mellen, 1998.

Gilson, Etienne. *History of Philosophy in the Middle Ages*. New York: Random House, 1955.

James, William. *Pragmatism: The Works of William James*. Cambridge: Harvard University Press, 1975.

McInerny, Ralph M. *Aquinas against the Averroists*. West Lafayette: Purdue University Press, 1993.

Sonneborn, Liz. *Averroes (Ibn Rushd): Muslim Scholar, Philosopher, and Physician of the Twelfth Century*. New York: Rosen Publishing, 2012.

van den Bergh, Simon. *Averroes' Tahafut al-tahafut: The Incoherence of the Incoherence*. 2 vols. London: Luzac, 1954.

31

MACHIAVELLI'S *PRINCE*

FROM PLATO'S *REPUBLIC* TO Thomas More's *Utopia*—
with a considerable "education of princes" literature in between—
theoreticians dealing with the governance of states have viewed the
matter from the angle of idealization. But *The Prince* by the Italian
statesman and political theorist Niccolò Machiavelli (1469–1527) put
a stop to all that and revolutionized the orientation of European
political thought.

Written in the form of counsel to a ruling prince, Machiavelli
advocates the hard line:

> A ruler who does not involve himself in military matters will
> not have the respect of his soldiers and so will not be able to trust
> them. He must therefore never cease to think about war and
> preparing for it, working at this even more in perception than
> in war itself. . . .
>
> Many writers have dreamed up republics and kingdoms that
> bear no resemblance to experience and never existed in reality;
> there is such a gap between how people actually live and how
> they ought to live that anyone who declines to behave as people
> do, in order to behave as they should, is schooling himself for

catastrophe and had better forget personal security: if you always want to play the good man in a world where most people are not good, you will have to learn to stop being good, at least when the occasion demands. . . .

If you are determined to have people think of you as generous, you'll have to be lavish in every possible way; naturally, a ruler who follows this policy will soon use up all this wealth to the point that, if he wants to keep his reputation, he will have to impose special taxes and do everything a ruler can to raise cash. His people will start to hate him and no one will respect him now he has no money. Since his generosity will have damaged the majority and benefitted only a few, he will be vulnerable to the first bad news, and the first real danger may well topple him. When he realizes this and tries to change his ways, he will immediately be accused of meanness. Since a ruler cannot be generous and show it without putting himself at risk, if he is sensible he will not mind getting a reputation for meanness.[1]

In the tension between an "idealistic" statesmanship, based on principles of morality, and the "realist" alternative of "raison d'état" and "might makes right," there is, after all, only a short step from the Machiavelli's exclusion of ethics from politics to von Clausewitz's dictum that warfare is a continuation of politics by other means.

Machiavelli has always been the poster child of hard-nosed political realism. And his resulting unsavory repute is betokened by the (doubtless spurious) idea at issue in the following distich:

Nick Machiavelli knew many a trick,
And gave his name to our "Old Nick."

To all appearances, Machiavelli's book maintained that political success trumps morality, that might makes right and that the end justifies the means. As Machiavelli depicted him, the effective prince makes the consolidation of power and extension of control his prime object. He would rather be feared than loved, seeing that the former is a more potent incentive to obedience. When necessary, he will be ruthless in dealing out punishments and penalties, seeing

---

1. Niccolò Machiavelli, *The Prince*, trans. Tim Parks (New York: Penguin, 2009), chaps. 14–16.

that this sort of thing is best got over with than dealt out in small doses extended over time. As Machiavelli saw it, a ruthless tyrant serves the state more effectively than a well-meaning weakling. (Witness Stalin or Tito.)

The Prince with its separation of ethics from politics made Machiavelli the most reviled political thinker since the Thrasymachus of Plato's *Republic*. It is, however, discussable whether Machiavelli himself approved and advocated the doctrines he described or merely reported that they reflect actual practice.

But in any case, Machiavelli's book was figured critically over the subsequent centuries in the ongoing conflict between political utopianism and realpolitik. And to this day the question of whether a political decider should leave personal morality at home when going to the office continues to be the subject of lively debate.

RELATED ANECDOTES

FURTHER READING

Machiavelli, Niccolò. *The Prince*. Translated by Tim Parks. New York: Penguin, 2009.

Parrish, John M. *Paradoxes of Political Ethics*. Cambridge: Cambridge University Press, 2007.

Strauss, Leo. *Thoughts on Machiavelli*. Chicago: University of Chicago Press, 1958.

PART

3

EARLY MODERNITY, 1500–1800

32

THE VALLADOLID DEBATE

AS SPAIN WAS COLONIZING the New World in the time of Philip II (1527–1598) there arose a bitter discord between the lucre-hungry conquistadors and the pious friars who, on orders of the king, always accompanied their explorations. The object of dispute was the status of the local natives, the indigenous peoples of the Americas. Were they—as the friars maintained—human beings with souls to be saved and lives to be integrated into the community of the church? Or were they—as the conquistadors preferred to think—like some of the larger hominids of Africa, sophisticated mammals available for labor in the gold and silver mines in much the same way that camels and oxen served as beasts of burden? Were they actually humans or were they to be seen as simply a somewhat more developed simian species?

When the friars who resisted the exploitation of the indigenous peoples of the Americas insisted on pressing their position, Philip II referred the matter to some of the best-available experts of the day—the cream of the crop among the theologians and academics of Spain. They assembled in 1550–1551 to resolve the issue in a scholastic debate at the University of Valladolid, whose focus was, in effect, the following proposition: *The indigenous natives of the New World are rational and ensouled beings who, as such, deserve the protection of king and church.*

The Salamanca-trained Dominican friar Bartolomé de las Casas—ever after dubbed the "Apostle of the Indies"—pleaded the friars' case with such eloquence and cogency that the assembled sages to their everlasting credit came down on the side of humanity. (Not that this made all that much difference to the hard men in charge of affairs in the Americas.)

The issue of transcended philosophical interest here is the question of the methodology of resolution. How to decide whether or not a creature seemingly capable of intelligent action—not obviously human and possibly even alien or android in nature—is or is not a fellow rational being? Is the matter to be addressed entirely in terms of analogies such as those at issue with the plea of Shylock in Shakespeare's *Merchant of Venice*?

> Hath not a Jew eyes? Hath not a Jew hands, organs, dimensions, senses, affections, passions? Fed with the same food, hurt with the same weapons, subject to the same diseases, healed by the same means, warmed and cooled by the same winter and summer, as a Christian is? If you prick us, do we not bleed? If you tickle us, do we not laugh? If you poison us, do we not die? And if you wrong us, shall we not revenge? If we are like you in the rest, we will resemble you in that.[1]

Many deep questions arise here. Does being human pivot on a close scrutiny of the extent of such analogies? Or is the operative factor simply a benefit of doubt as long as there is reasonable room for it? Does the weight of such determinations rest on the factual or on the ethical balance of the scale? Should it be necessary to press the analogy of modus operandi ever onward into greater detail—or should even a little of it suffice to settle matters by bringing the principle of Christian charity to bear? The Valladolid episode provides much food for thought along these lines, inviting reflection about just what it takes to qualify creatures as actually human.

---

1. William Shakespeare, *The Merchant of Venice*, ed. Jonathan Bate and Eric Rasmussen (Basingstoke: Palgrave Macmillan, 2010), act 3, scene 1.

RELATED ANECDOTES

FURTHER READING

de las Casas, Bartolomé. *A Brief Account of the Destruction of the Indies.* In his *Witness: Writings of Bartolomé de las Casas.* Edited and translated by George Sanderlin. Maryknoll: Orbis, 1993.

Prescott, William H. *The History of the Reign of Philip the Second, King of Spain.* London: Routledge, 1855.

Shakespeare, William. *The Merchant of Venice.* Edited by Jonathan Bate and Eric Rasmussen. Basingstoke: Palgrave Macmillian, 2010.

33

MORE'S *UTOPIA*

THOMAS MORE (1478-1535) WAS an English lawyer, statesman, and philosopher—as well as martyr owing to his clash with Henry VIII's divorcement plans. Canonized as a saint by the Church of Rome, More's claim to lasting fame also rests on his imaginative work *Utopia*—an imaginary state where people thrive in well-being, virtue, and fulfillment. His ingenious speculation added a new word to European vocabulary.

While More's utopia retained the hierarchical structure of the old regime in its Renaissance version, it incorporated a system of noblesse oblige, where subordination from below is softened by paternalistic consideration from above. In his imagined domain:

> No magistrate is either haughty or fearful. Fathers they are called, and like fathers they behave. The citizens, as it is their duty, willingly pay to them due honor without any compulsion. Nor is the prince himself known from others by his apparel, or by a crown or diadem or cap of maintenance, but by a little sheaf of corn carried before him; as a taper of wax is borne

before a bishop, whereby only he is known. They have but few laws. For people so instructed and trained very few suffice. Yea, the thing they chiefly disapprove among other nations is that innumerable books of laws and expositions of the same are not sufficient. . . .

But in Utopia every man is learned in the law. For, as I said, they have very few laws; and the plainer and more blunt that any interpretation is, that they approve as most just. For all laws, they say, are made and published only for the purpose that by them every man should be put in remembrance of his duty. But the crafty and subtle interpretation of them can put very few in that remembrance (for they are but few who understand them), whereas the simple, the plain/and literal meaning of the laws is open to every man.[1]

The state, as More conceived it, allots power for the purposes of service rather than exploitation, with personal submission compensated for by the general benefit of well-intentioned governance.

Interestingly, More's ideal state is in one way an inversion of Plato's. With Plato, personal virtue is largely the product of arrangements managed by the state. With More the state is benign because its citizens are virtuous. And the jury is still out on the question of whether it takes good citizens to make for a good state or whether well-conceived public policies are a requisite for having a duly right-minded citizenry. Moreover, the historic quarrel of theoreticians of public affairs between the More-oriented idealists, whose hopeful vision looks to what is theoretically possible, and the Machiavelli-oriented realists, who look to the seemingly unavoidable actualities, does not look to be headed for an early resolution.

RELATED ANECDOTES

---

1.   Thomas More, *Utopia*, book II.

FURTHER READING

Ackroyd, Peter. *The Life of Thomas More*. New York: Nan A. Talese, 1998.

Guy, John. *Thomas More*. New York: Oxford University Press, 2000.

Manuel, Frank Edward, and Fritzie Prigohzy Manuel. *Utopian Thought in the Western World*. Cambridge: Belknap Press, 1979.

More, Thomas. *Utopia*. Translated by Dominic Baker-Smith. London: Penguin, 2012.

Sullivan, E. D. S., ed. *The Utopian Vision*. San Diego: San Diego State University Press, 1980.

34

DR. FAUSTUS'S BARGAIN

THE STORY OF DR. FAUSTUS and his bargain with Satan was launched on a promising literary career in the play of that name by Christopher Marlowe (1564—1593). In briefest outline its plot ran as follows: Distressed with the limited range and utility of human knowledge, and urged on by an inner yearning for greater power, Dr. Faustus, a great German scholar, sells his soul to the Devil to overcome these limitations. But even this yields no real satisfaction of spirit and in the end Faustus not only regrets but also retracts and finds pardon from an accepting God for whom those who truly repent of sin can obtain forgiveness.

A striking feature of Marlowe's play is that here, as in Goethe's great reworking of the same theme, the Devil is every bit as interesting a figure as the hero Faustus. And it is the Devil, rather than Faustus, who is the bearer of the key lesson that the ultimate punishment does not reside in the physical torments of the nether regions but in the mental torment of alienation from God. For when Faustus asks how it is that Mephistopheles has come out of hell, he replies:

> Why this is hell, nor am I out of it.
> Think'st thou that I, who saw the face of God,

And tasted the eternal joys of heaven,
Am not tormented with ten thousand hells
In being deprived of everlasting bliss?[1]

Subsequently immortalized in Goethe's wonderful drama, the story of Dr. Faustus has long enjoyed the attention of philosophers—unsurprisingly so, seeing that it vividly illustrates a number of notable weaknesses of the human condition, specifically

- our dedication to self-interest
- our tendency to prioritize near-term benefit over long-term considerations with its yen for immediate gratification and impatience for the realization of good things
- our prioritizing material and worldly over spiritual goods
- our tendency to subordinate judgment to desire
- the weakness of our will in choosing the worse while acknowledging the better

Dr. Faustus is a member of a larger family of those who illustrate the futility and frustrations of a life devoted to the acquisition of riches, be it the riches of the treasure chamber (King Midas), of the ballroom (Jay Gatsby), of the bedchamber (Don Juan), of the dining room (Edward VII), or of the study (Faustus himself). The object lesson throughout is that a satisfying life is not achievable through ardent dedication to worldly goods (of whatever kind). After all, we have only one life to live, one single life-shaping opportunity at our disposal. And none of those objectives affords a means to real satisfaction—to "rational contentment" in this regard—none points us toward a life that a sensible person would be prepared to admire and emulate. As this confronts us with the daunting and depressing prospect that reality is indifferent—and perhaps even antagonistic—to the good: that value has no place in the world's scheme of things.

The Dr. Faustus story also admits of the graphic interpretation that does not envision an actual "deal with the devil" but rather sees Faustus as a quintessential human, "bedeviled" by our natural weakness in yielding to the lower and crasser side of our complex nature. The crux here is not philosophy's often manifested discord

---

1.   Christopher Marlowe, *Dr. Faustus* (London: Macmillan, 1969).

at the communal level of interpersonal rivalry but rather the no less commonly manifested discord at the intrapersonal level of competing inclinations—the person-internal dissonance of different and competing aspects of our nature.

Moreover, the fact of Satan's prominence in the story is also significant in making the philosophically significant point that in this world we humans are engaged in grappling with unfriendly potencies above and beyond our powers to control—individually and collectively alike.

The prominence of Faustian themes on philosophy's agenda provides a reminder of the diversified nature of philosophical concern and inspiration. Some philosophers find the grist to their mill in scientific inquiry, others in public affairs, and yet others in literature and cultural artifice. And so for some, observation is the crux, but for others, imagination. And no one can claim a monopoly. The field can, should, and does provide room to accommodate different lines of approach.

RELATED ANECDOTES

FURTHER READING

Goethe, J. W. *Faust: A Tragedy*. Edinburgh: W. Blackwood, 1834.

Marlowe, Christopher. *Dr. Faustus*. London: Macmillan, 1969.

Ruickbie, Leo. *Faustus: The Life and Times of a Renaissance Magician*. Stroud: History, 2009.

35

HOBBES'S *LEVIATHAN*

THE VALIDITY OF STATE power has been an issue on the philosophical agenda since Plato's day. And here fact and fiction alike confront us with the social skeptic's question: "Why should I conform to the accepted ways and obey the established rules? Why should I not do as I please and be a law unto myself? Why should I concede to others the right to 'lay down the law' to me, acknowledging their authority to circumscribe what I may or may not do?"

The English philosopher Thomas Hobbes (1588–1679) is especially prominent among those who have grappled with these issues. Regarding the state as a powerful being, a sort of super-man or Leviathan, he projected the following line of thought:

> [In] a time of Warre, where every man is Enemy to every man; the same is consequent to the time, wherein men live without other security, than what their own strength, and their own invention shall furnish them withall. In such condition, there is no place for Industry; because the fruit thereof is uncertain: and consequently no Culture of the Earth; no Navigation, nor use of the commodities that may be imported by Sea;

no commodious Building; no Instruments of moving, and removing such things as require much force; no Knowledge of the face of the Earth; no account of Time; no Arts; no Letters; no Society; and which is worst of all, continuall feare, and danger of violent death; And the life of man, solitary, poore, nasty, brutish, and short.[1]

The state lives a life of its own. It is an organism of sorts: the populace is its "body politic"; the governing apparatus its "head." And people should (and generally do) accept what they find in place because the alternative is destabilization—chaos, a "war of all against all."

And in such a situation everyone will lose out. Without rules of the road, there will be traffic snarls and collisions. Without orderly queuing, there will be shoving and tussling. Without an orderly transfer of property, there can be no security of ownership. Without social order, there will be a condition of might makes right that renders virtually everyone a loser.

Hobbes's rationale for acknowledging the "powers that be" ran effectively as follows: Consider the alternative. Ask yourself what sort of situation you would confront in a society where everyone proceeded to be a law unto themselves. The result will be a free-for-all subject to the principle of every man for himself. Your chances of a satisfying life would be next to nil. In forming an orderly queue I forego my chance of early access to establish an orderly process from which I—and everybody—profits.

As Hobbes saw it, there is no single theoretical basis for authority: neither dynastic legitimacy ("the divine right of being") nor established power is it (Machiavellian "might makes right"). In the final analysis the matter is one of what people will accept and acquiesce to, what they are willing to "come to terms with" owing to its superiority over unpleasant alternatives.

In 1792, some 100 years after Hobbes's *Leviathan*, Jean-Jacques Rousseau (1712–1778) published his classic *Émile*, which effectively turned Hobbes upside down. Hobbes taught that civic society does and should function to restrain and canalize the primal selfishness

---

1. Thomas Hobbes, *Leviathan*, ed. Richard Tuck (Cambridge: Cambridge University Press, 1991), part 1, chap. 13.

and harmful instincts of primitive natural man; Rousseau, by contrast, regarded primitive natural man as a paradigm of goodness and viewed civic society as corrupting these merits and impelling man into discord, strife, and wickedness.

Rousseau's view of the state was thus the inverse of that of Hobbes's. He wrote: "Man was born free, but is everywhere in bondage. Most any man believes himself the master of his fellows, but is nevertheless more of a slave than they. How did this change *from freedom into bondage* come about?"[2] As Rousseau saw it, the state is not the controller of social discord but its source. In the story of *Émile*, Rousseau expounds his paradigm of natural human virtue: "Everything is good as it leaves the hands of the Author of things; everything degenerates in the hands of man."[3]

In due course, the German philosopher G. W. F. Hegel (1770–1831) added another twist here. In roughest outline, his view of the matter was something like this: The state is not the product of the contract or acquiescence of its citizens, it has a life of its own and is a force in its own right—even as a migration is more than various individuals' decisions to relocate. And the state is not only the grantor of laws and order but also the matrix of a civil society that provides for its members a framework for constructive action and productive interaction. Rights, claims, opportunities of all sorts exist only because the state is there to create and foster them. (Think of how chaotic claims to land would be without the coordinating intervention of the state and how difficult things would be without the money it provides as a medium of exchange.) As Hegel saw it, the state is an indispensable source of constructive resources for the benefit of its citizenry. It exists not merely to reduce harm (as per Hobbes) but also to provide for positive benefit.

This controversy about the relation of man to civil society and the role or place of organized institutions in human affairs has been a key sector of philosophical controversy from Plato to the present

2. Jean-Jacques Rousseau, *The Social Contract*, trans. W. Kendall (South Bend: Gateway, 1954), book 1, chap. 1.

3. Jean-Jacques Rousseau, *Émile*, trans. Allan Bloom (New York: Basic, 1979), 37.

day. And neither in philosophy nor in practical politics has there ever been agreement about the right balance between too much and too little intrusion of the state into the lives of its people.

RELATED ANECDOTES

FURTHER READING

Hobbes, Thomas. *Leviathan*. Edited by Richard Tuck. Cambridge: Cambridge University Press, 1991.

Rousseau, Jean-Jacques. *Émile*. Translated by Allan Bloom. New York: Basic, 1979.

Rousseau, Jean-Jacques. *The Social Contract*. Translated by W. Kendall. South Bend: Gateway, 1954.

36

DESCARTES'S DECEIVER

IN HIS QUEST FOR a factual claim of whose truth is absolutely certain, René Descartes (1596–1650), the French thinker often called "the father of modern philosophy," had the ingenious idea of beginning at the other end, not with truth but with falsity and not with knowledge but with deception. Thus in his *Meditations on First Philosophy*, Descartes envisioned a wicked and powerful deceiver whom he supposed to dedicate his powers to deceive him and to upset the entire applecart of his knowledge and convictions:

> I shall then suppose, not that God who is supremely good and the fountain of truth, but some evil genius not less powerful than deceitful, has employed his whole energies in deceiving me; I shall consider that the heavens, the earth, colours, figures, sound, and all other external things are nought but the illusions and dreams of which this genius has availed himself in order to lay traps for my credulity; I shall consider myself as having no hands, no eyes, no flesh, no blood, nor any senses, yet falsely believing myself to possess all these things.[1]

---

1.   René Descartes, *Meditations in First Philosophy*, "Meditation I," trans. E. S. Haldane and G. R. T. Ross (Cambridge: Cambridge University Press, 1931), 148.

Can anything be salvaged from the wreckage that such an assumption leaves in its seemingly all-destructive wake?

Descartes was certain that one fact would remain untouched and secure: the fact of his own existence.

> I suppose, then, that all the things that I see are false; I persuade myself that nothing has ever existed of all that my fallacious memory represents to me. I consider that I possess no senses; I imagine that body, figure, extension, movement and place are but the fictions of my mind. What, then, can be esteemed as true? . . . I myself, am I not at least something? But I have already denied that I had senses and body. Yet I hesitate, for what follows from that? Am I so dependent on body and senses that I cannot exist without these? But I was persuaded that there was nothing in all the world, that there was no heaven, no earth, that there were no minds, nor any bodies: was I not then likewise persuaded that I did not exist? Not at all; of a surety I myself did exist since I persuaded myself of something (or merely because I thought of something). But there is some deceiver or other, very powerful and very cunning, whoever employs his ingenuity in deceiving me. Then without doubt I exist also if he deceives me, and let him deceive me as much as he will, he can never cause me to be nothing so long as I think that I am something. So that after reflecting well and carefully examining all things, one must come to the definite conclusion that this proposition: I am, I exist, is necessarily true each time that I pronounce it, or that I mentally conceive it.[2]

Unfortunately, however, Descartes's approach leaves open a problem as big as that which it tries to resolve. For consider the following two contentions:

- There is a cat on the mat.
- I am under the impression that there is a cat on the mat. (Or "I take there to be a cat on the mat.")

Clearly the second stands fast and secure. No matter how deceived you may be in the matter of cats and mats, that second subjectively self-oriented statement survives intact. But that first contention is

---

2. Descartes, *Meditations in First Philosophy*, 149–50.

something else again. Here there is many a possible slip between the cup of reality and the lip of apprehension.

But unfortunately that secure item is merely a self-referential claim about oneself rather than about any feature of the external world. We confront the awkward fact that the claim is about you and that the existence and reality of the world's things is left entirely out of sight. And herein lies a big difficulty both for Descartes and for the multitude of modern "evidentist" thinkers who follow in his wake. When all that there is in the premises are facts about oneself—one's thought's regresses, connections, and so on—then reasoning alone cannot transport one outside this realm. When we operate entirely from within the realm of self-oriented subjectivity, then all we can ever securely extract from this will remain subjective and without access to an objectively self-independent world order.

And so Descartes soon found himself painted into a corner from whence only an appeal to God could possibly extract him. And those of his successors, who—like most moderns—felt reluctant to call on God for philosophical support, soon found themselves resorting to problematic expedients like that of constituting cats out of cat impressions. The Cartesian demarche embarked modern philosophy on an endeavor to construct an objective reality out of subjective materials. And—unsurprisingly—this has turned out to be a virtual impossibility. In the eyes of his posterity, Descartes's seemingly promising turn inward to the self proved to be a philosophical dead end.

RELATED ANECDOTES

15. Plato's Knowledge   44
39. Calderon's Dream   118
93. Simon's Satisficing   260

FURTHER READING

Descartes, René. *Discourse on Method.* Translated by Desmond M. Clarke. New York: Penguin, 2000.

Descartes, René. *Meditations in First Philosophy.* Translated by E. S. Haldane and G. R. T. Ross. Cambridge: Cambridge University Press, 1931.

Rescher, Nicholas. *Scepticism.* Oxford: Blackwell, 1980.

37

DESCARTES'S ERGO

DESCARTES BECAME ETERNALLY FAMOUS for his dictum "I think therefore I am" (*Cogito ergo sum*). He had much work for this dictum to do: "I noticed that even when I wanted to think all things false, it was absolutely essential that the 'I' who thought this should be somewhat, and remarking that this truth 'I think, therefore I am' was, so certain and so assured that all the most extravagant suppositions brought forward by the sceptics were incapable of shaking it, I came to the conclusion that I could receive it without scruple as the first principle of the Philosophy for which I was seeking."[1] In taking self-apprehension as the model instance for knowledge, Cartesian philosophy effectively inverted the Copernican Revolution in science. For while Copernicus expelled us humans from an Aristotelian centrality in the world of nature, Descartes firmly emplaced us at the very center of the *cognitive* realm.

In their philosophizing the ancients wanted to know how matters stand in the world; the moderns since Descartes focus their

---

1. René Descartes, *Discourse on Method*, trans. Desmond M. Clarke (New York: Penguin, 2000), part 4.

inquiries on how we ourselves can and should proceed in explaining this issue. Their emphasis shifted from "What is the case?" to "How can we get to know what the case is?," where the center of concern is now moved from being to knowing, from ontology to epistemology. They refocused attention from the object of investigation to its practitioners, and thereby ultimately to the individuals in whose activities any investigating must be grounded.

The prime example of the philosophical egocentrism that evolved in this way was the English philosopher G. E. Moore.

> I have asserted that I do have certain perceptions, which it is very unlikely I should have, unless some other person had certain particular perceptions; that, for instance, it is very unlikely I should be having precisely those perceptions which I am now having unless someone else were hearing the sound of my voice. And I now wish to ask: What reason have I for supposing that this is unlikely? What reason has any of us for supposing that any such proposition is true? And I mean by "having a reason" precisely what I formerly meant. I mean: What other proposition do I know, which would not be true, unless my perception were connected with someone else's perception, in the manner in which I asserted them to be connected? Here again I am asking for *a good reason*; and am not asking a psychological question with regard to origin. Here again I am not asking for a reason, in the strict sense of Formal Logic; I am merely asking for a proposition which would probably not be true, unless what I asserted were true. Here again I am asking for some proposition of a kind which *each* of us believes; I am asking: What reason has *each* of us for believing that some of his perceptions are connected with particular perceptions of other people in the manner I asserted?— for believing that he would not have certain perceptions that he does have, unless some other person had certain particular perceptions? And here again I am asking for a *reason*.[2]

The presumption that underpins much modern philosophy is that in regard to philosophical thinking oneself is typical, paradigmatic, representative; that what holds for *me* holds for *us*. This of

2. George Edward Moore, "Objects of Perception," *Philosophical Studies* (London: Routledge and Kegan Paul, 1922), 48–49.

course means that one must take as the central focus those aspects of oneself that are general and generic rather than personal, eccentric, and idiosyncratic. And this is something that is a good deal easier said than done.

To be sure, one promising pathway that leads beyond subjectivity is afforded by language. After all, communication is predicated on coordination, commonality. (At this point Ludwig Wittgenstein's rejection of the idea of a "[totally] private language" becomes pivotal.) And so, the human individual and the human mind and its instrumentalities—above all *language*—now came to the center of the philosophical stage. And this "linguistic turn" has meant that it is artifice rather than nature—and language rather than impersonal reality—that has become the focus of much modern philosophizing.

RELATED ANECDOTES

49. Hume's Self-Seeking **146**
85. Sci-Fi Psychology **239**

FURTHER READING

Descartes, René. *Discourse on Method.* Translated by Desmond M. Clarke. New York: Penguin, 2000.

Moore, George Edward. *Philosophical Studies.* London: Routledge, 1922.

Rorty, Richard. *The Linguistic Turn.* Chicago: University of Chicago Press, 1967.

Ryle, Gilbert. *The Concept of Mind.* New York: Hutchinson's University Library, 1949.

Urmson, J. O. *Philosophical Analysis: Its Development between the Two World Wars.* Oxford: Clarendon, 1956. See especially references to Ludwig Wittgenstein.

38

DESCARTES'S FIRM FOUNDATION

IN HIS *DISCOURSE ON METHOD*, Descartes depicted philosophizing as a construction project. He wrote:

> [Sometimes] the houses in a town are rased to the ground for the sole reason that the town is to be rebuilt in another fashion, with streets made more beautiful; but more commonly people cause their own houses to be knocked down in order to rebuild them, being forced so to do where there is danger of the houses falling of themselves because their foundations are not secure. From such examples I argued to myself that. . . . as regards all the opinions which up to this time I had embraced, I thought I could not do better than endeavor once for all to sweep them completely away, so that they might later be replaced, whether by others which were more secure or by the same, when I had made them conform to the uniformity of a rational scheme.[1]

Yet Descartes was not just a philosopher but also a mathematician, and his ideal model for scholarly exposition was a mathematical

---

1. René Descartes, *Discourse on Method*, trans. Desmond M. Clarke (New York: Penguin, 2000), part 2.

treatise on the order of Euclid's elements. In such a treatment, of course, the reasoning proceeds step by small and individually obvious step to draw significant—and sometimes unexpected— conclusions from a basis of experientially validated givens. The starting point here is always something so "clear and distinct" that its truth is obvious and evident. The overall process of reasoning is thus one of erecting upon a secure and in itself totally unproblematic foundation a larger structure of well-secured information.

But here as in any piece of deductive reasoning, the conclusion is no more secure and certain than the least secure and certain of the premises. So the absolute security of the ultimate premises becomes essential. The entire structure of thought must rest on a firm and uncontestable foundation.

However, while this "foundationalist" view of cognitive substantiation seems to hold good in mathematics, it is very questionable whether it is applicable elsewhere. In many fields of inquiry we actually do not set out from a small but secure starter set, but rather we determine acceptability within a large and amorphous manifold of plausibility through best-fit considerations. And with this methodology of coherent harmonization, the difference between the acceptable and the unacceptable becomes clear only at the end of the process—not at its beginning.

RELATED ANECDOTES

FURTHER READING

Descartes, René. *Discourse on Method*. Translated by Desmond M. Clarke. New York: Penguin, 2000.

Descartes, René. *Meditations in First Philosophy*. Translated by E. S. Haldane and G. R. T. Ross. Cambridge: Cambridge University Press, 1931.

Rescher, Nicholas. *Epistemology*. Albany: SUNY Press, 2003.

Sosa, Ernest, Jaegwon Kim, Jeremy Fantl, and Matthew McGrath, eds. *Epistemology: An Anthology*. Oxford: Blackwell, 2008.

39

CALDERON'S DREAM

THE IDEA THAT THE entire life we take ourselves to be living might in reality be only a dream has origins that are lost in the impenetrable mists of antiquity. The thought is adumbrated in the Hindu belief that this world of ours is *maya*, a mere illusion. And it recurs in Plato's allegory of the cave,[1] whose cave dwellers—we denizens of this world—must come to realize that what they experience is not reality but a mere seeming—a "meaningless illusion," a world of shadows. The idea subsequently gained considerable traction in the seventeenth century, being prominent in the thematics of the celebrated play *Life Is a Dream* (*La vida es sueño*) by the Spanish poet and dramatist Calderon de la Barca (1600–1681), which reflected the philosophical thought experimentation of Descartes's *Discourse on Method*.

We have here one of those philosophical hypotheses that, like that of solipsistic solitude, cannot be refuted by empirical evidence but nevertheless cannot secure any cognitive conviction.

---

1. Plato, *The Republic*, VIII, 514A.

Perhaps the best that can be done here is to adopt the position of G. W. Leibniz, which ran as follows:

> Let us now see by what criteria we may know which phenomena are real. We may judge this both from the phenomenon itself and from the phenomena which are antecedent and consequent to it as well. We conclude it from the phenomenon itself if it is vivid, complex, and internally coherent [*congruum*]. It will be vivid if its qualities, such as light, color, and warmth, appear intense enough. It will be complex if these qualities are varied and support us in undertaking many experiments and new observations; for example, if we experience in a phenomenon not merely colors but also sounds, odors, and qualities of taste and touch, and this both in the phenomenon as a whole and in its various parts which we can further treat according to causes. Such a long chain of observations is usually begun by design and selectively and usually occurs neither in dreams nor in those imaginings which memory or fantasy present, in which the image is mostly vague and disappears while we are examining it. A phenomenon will be coherent when it consists of many phenomena, for which a reason can be given either within themselves or by some sufficiently simple hypothesis common to them; next, it is coherent if it conforms to the customary nature of other phenomena which have repeatedly occurred to us, so that its parts have the same position, order, and outcome in relation to the phenomenon which similar phenomena have had. Otherwise phenomena will be suspect, for if we were to see men moving through the air astride the hippogryphs of Ariostus, it would, I believe, make us uncertain whether we were dreaming or awake. But this criterion can be referred back to another general class of tests drawn from preceding phenomena. The present phenomenon must be coherent with these if, namely, it preserves the same consistency or if a reason can be supplied for it from preceding phenomena or if all together are coherent with the same hypothesis, as if with a common cause. But certainly a most valid criterion is a consensus with the whole sequence of life, especially if many others affirm the same thing to be coherent with their phenomena also, for it is not only probable but certain, as I will show directly, that other

substances exist which are similar to us. Yet the most powerful criterion of the reality of phenomena, sufficient even by itself, is success in predicting future phenomena from past and present ones, whether that prediction is based upon a reason, upon a hypothesis that was previously successful, or upon the customary consistency of things as observed previously. Indeed, even if this whole life were said to be only a dream, and the visible world only a phantasm, I should call this dream or this phantasm real enough if we were never deceived by it when we make good use of reason.[2]

The contrast between authentic experience and dream experience is itself perfectly appropriate, but this difference cannot be transmuted into a distinction between our experience as a whole and something wholly outside and beyond it. The contrast between how things are and how things seem is not one between seeming and non-seeming but one between correct and incorrect seeming: in drawing it, we remain within the realm of seeming.

Consider an analogy. The distinction between meaningful discourse and gibberish can be implemented only *within* the discursive realm. To try to apply it to distinguish between the linguistically discussable and something outside this communicative range is a step into incoherence and unintelligibility. Analogously, the idea of sleep makes sense only where there is a manifold of waking experience to stand in contrast. The idea that the whole of our experience might *all* be sleep makes no sense because it saws off the limb of its own contrast between drawing and voting experience.

There may be good reasons for skepticism regarding what Bertrand Russell called "our knowledge of the external world," but the dream hypothesis is not one of these.

RELATED ANECDOTES

36. Descartes's Deceiver   **110**
99. Searle's Chinese Room   **276**

FURTHER READING

2.   G. W. Leibniz, *G. W. Leibniz: Collected Papers and Letters*, ed. L. E. Loemker (Dordrecht: D. Reidel, 1969), 363–64.

Armas, Frederick A. de. *The Prince in the Tower: Perceptions of* La Vida Es Sueño. Cranbury: Associated University Presses, 1993.

Barca, Pedro Calderon de la. *Life's a Dream: A Prose Translation.* Edited and translated by Michael Kidd. Boulder: University of Colorado Press, 2004.

Descartes, René. *Discourse on Method.* Translated by Desmond M. Clarke. New York: Penguin, 2000.

Descartes, René. *Meditations in First Philosophy.* Translated by E. S. Haldane and G. R. T. Ross. Cambridge: Cambridge University Press, 1931.

Leibniz, G. W. "On the Method of Distinguishing Real from Imaginary Phenomena." In *G. W. Leibniz: Collected Papers and Letters*, edited by L. E. Loemker, 363–66. Dordrecht: D. Reidel, 1969.

PASCAL'S WAGER

DURING THE LAST FIVE years of his brief life, the French philosopher and theologian Blaise Pascal (1623–1662) wrote a collection of notes for a projected *Apology for the Christian Religion*. And here in a famous passage he wrote:

> Let us examine this point and declare: "Either God exists, or He does not." To which view shall we incline? Reason cannot decide for us one way or the other: we are separated by an infinite gulf. At the extremity of this infinite distance a game is in progress, where either heads or tails may turn up. What will you wager? According to reason you cannot bet either way; according to reason you can defend neither proposition.
>
> So do not attribute error to those who have made a choice; for you know nothing about it.
>
> "No; I will not blame them for having made this choice, but for having made one at all; for since he who calls heads and he who calls tails are equally at fault, both are wrong. The right thing is not to wager at all." Yes; but a bet must be laid. There is no option: you have joined the game. Which will you choose, then? Let us weigh the gain and the loss involved in wagering

that God exists. Let us estimate these two possibilities; if you win, you win all; if you lose, you lose nothing. Wager then, without hesitation, that He does exist. For us there is an infinity of infinitely happy life to win, one chance of winning against a finite number of chances of losing, and what you stake is finite. That removes all doubt as to choice; wherever the infinite is to be won, and there is not an infinity of chances of loss against the chance of winning, there are no two ways about it: you must risk all. . . . But I am so made that I cannot believe. What then do you wish me to do? . . . That is true. But understand at least that your inability to believe is the result of your passions; for although reason (now) inclines you to believe, you cannot do so. Try therefore to convince yourself, not by piling up proofs of God, but by subduing your passions. . . . You desire to attain faith, but you do not know the way. You would like to cure yourself of unbelief, and you ask for remedies. Learn from those who were once bound and gagged like you, and who now stake all that they possess. They are men who know the road that you desire to follow, and who have been cured of a sickness of which you desire to be cured. Follow the way by which they set out.[1]

This approach represents a remarkable transformation in the perspective of religious apologetics—a revision that might be called "Pascal's shift in theological argumentation." For what we have here is clearly a move away from factual considerations that purport to demonstrate the existence of God (in the manner of Aquinas's "Five Ways") to a different style of *practical* argumentation, geared not to a theoretical argument for the existence of God as an ontological fact but to a practical resolution regarding what we ought to believe. The salient feature of the argument is thus its recourse to praxis and to prudence: to the realization of our best interests.

And Pascal was perfectly content to have his reasoning pivot on self-interest because, in light of his apologetic aims, he viewed this as initially necessary to reach the sort of person whom he wants to persuade. There are also, of course, nonprudential grounds for belief, faith, and hope—reasons that are not crassly self-interested and whose inherent superiority is not to be denied. But one must walk

---

1. Blaise Pascal, *Pensées*, trans. A. J. Krailsheimer (New York: Penguin, 1995).

before one can run—and one must make brittle iron before one can make firm steel. The less noble incentives to religious faith (or to morality, for that matter) are by no means contemptible in themselves precisely because they can provide helpful stepping-stones toward better things. For, as Pascal saw it, it is not sensible to condemn fastidiously the less-than-ideal helps that offer themselves along the way of life's journey. An exclusionary all-or-nothing ideology is neither very sensible nor very admirable.

RELATED ANECDOTES

34. Dr. Faustus's Bargain   **103**
93. Simon's Satisficing   **260**

FURTHER READING

Hunter, Graeme. *Pascal the Philosopher.* Toronto: University of Toronto Press, 2013.

Jorden, Jeff. *Pascal's Wager: Pragmatism Arguments and Belief in God.* Oxford: Oxford University Press, 2007.

Pascal, Blaise. *Pensées.* Translated by A. J. Krailsheimer. New York: Penguin, 1995.

Rescher, Nicholas. *Pascal's Wager.* Notre Dame: University of Notre Dame Press, 1985.

41

SPINOZA'S WORM AND LEIBNIZ'S LEAP

IN WRITING TO A fellow scholar, the Judeo-Dutch philosopher Benedict Spinoza (1632–1677) offered a highly instructive illustration:

> Suppose, he wrote, that a parasitic worm living in the bloodstream tried to make sense of its surroundings: from the point of view of the worm, each drop of blood would appear as an independent whole and not as a part of a total system. The worm would not recognize that each drop behaves as it does in virtue of the nature of the bloodstream as a whole. But in fact the nature of the blood can be understood only in the context of a larger system in which blood, lymph, and other fluids interact: and this system in turn is a part of a still larger whole. If we men begin with the bodies that surround us in nature and treat them as independent wholes, the relation between which is contingent and given, then we shall be in error precisely as the worm is in error. We must grasp the system as a whole before we can hope to grasp the nature of the part, since the nature of the part is determined by its role in the total system.[1]

---

1. Cited in Alasdair MacIntyre, "Spinoza," in *The Encyclopedia of Philosophy*, ed. Paul Edwards (New York: Macmillan, 1967), 7: 531.

This point of view is of particular importance for philosophy. For insofar as such a perspective is right, our inquiries into facts cannot be confined to the local area of immediate thematic environs of the contention but will have to involve its more remote ramifications as well. Thus the absolute idealist for whom "time is unreal" cannot appropriately just write off the ethicist's interest in future eventuations (as regards, for example, the situation that will obtain when the time to make good a promise arrives)—or the political philosopher's concern for the well-being of future generations. And the materialist cannot ignore the boundary-line issues involved in the moral question of why pointlessly damaging a computer that one owns is merely foolish, while pointlessly injuring a developed animal is actually wicked.

The approach leads to the epistemic doctrine of semantical coherentism, which sees concepts as intelligible only in their systemic setting. The proper understanding of ideas demands the wisdom of hindsight. An idea can only be adequately understood in retrospect after it becomes possible to see just where it leads. But this impetus to inclusive holism creates problems of its own.

Understanding a totality is easier said than done. For as Spinoza's critic G. W. Leibniz (1646–1716) observed:

> Let us imagine the book on the Elements of Geometry to have been eternal, one copy always being made from another; then it is clear that though we can give a reason for the present book based on the preceding book from which it was copied, we can never arrive at a complete reason, no matter how many books we may assume in the past, for one can always wonder why such books should have existed at all times; why there should be books at all, and why they should be written in this way. What is true of books is true also of the different states of the world; every subsequent state is somehow copied from the preceding one (although according to certain laws of change). No matter how far we may have gone back to earlier states, therefore, we will never discover in them a full reason why there should be a world at all, and why it should be such as it is.
>
> Even if we should imagine the world to be eternal, therefore, the reason for it would clearly have to be sought elsewhere, since we would still be assuming nothing but a succession of states,

in any one of which we can find no sufficient reason, [for the whole]. . . . The reasons for the world therefore lie in something extramundane, different from the chain of states or series of things whose aggregate constitutes the world. And so we must go from physical or hypothetical necessity, which determines later things in the world from earlier ones, to something which has absolute or metaphysical necessity, for which no reason can be given. . . . So there must exist something which is distinct from the plurality of beings, or from the world [that accounts for the entirety of its content.][2]

So if Leibniz is right, and a totality as such can only be properly explained and understood from an external vantage point, then we worm-like inquirers are condemned to proceed by conjecture and analogy to come to terms with the paradox that a proper understanding of a whole requires a proper understanding of its parts— and (alas!) also the converse.

RELATED ANECDOTES

61. Saxe's Puzzling Elephant   **176**
82. Collingwood's Presuppositions   **228**

FURTHER READING

Della Rocca, Michael. *Spinoza*. London: Routledge, 2008.
Popkin, Richard. *Spinoza*. Oxford: One World, 2004.
Pruss, Alexander. *The Principle of Sufficient Reason*. Cambridge: Cambridge University Press, 2006.
Rescher, Nicholas. *Philosophical Reasoning*. Oxford: Blackwell, 2001.

---

2.   G. W. Leibniz, "On the Radical Organization of Things," *Philosophical Papers and Letters*, 2nd ed., ed. L. E. Loemker (Dordrecht: D. Reidel, 1969), 486–91.

42

HUYGENS'S
PLANETARIANS

IN THE SEVENTEENTH CENTURY, the Dutch scientist and scholar Christiaan Huygens (1629–1695) posed questions about extraterrestrial intelligences that had to wait for almost three hundred years to gain real traction in the world of thought. He wrote:

> For 'tis a very ridiculous opinion that the common people have got among them, that it is impossible a rational Soul should dwell in any other shape than ours. . . . This can proceed from nothing but the Weakness, Ignorance, and rejoice of Men; as well as the humane Figure being the handsomest and most excellent of all others, when indeed it's nothing but a being accustomed to that figure that makes me think so, and a conceit . . . that no shape or colour can be so good as our own.[1]

But while Huygens was prepared to accept the prospect that his intelligent alien "Planetarians" had a *physical* form very different from ours, he took the line that their *cognitive* operations had to be very

---

1. Christiaan Huygens, *Cosmotheoros: The Celestial Worlds Discovered—New Conjectures Concerning the Planetary Worlds, Their Inhabitants and Productions* (London: F. Cass, 1968), 76–77.

similar. As he saw it, their logic, their mathematics, their science, and even their morality had to be substantially the same.

There is, no doubt, a certain charm to the idea of companionship. It would be comforting to reflect that, however estranged we are from them in other ways, those alien minds of distant planets share *science* with us at any rate and are our fellow travelers on a common journey of inquiry. Our yearning for companionship and contact runs deep. It might be pleasant to think of ourselves not only as colleagues but also as junior collaborators whom other, wiser minds might be able to help along the way. Even as many in sixteenth-century Europe looked to those strange seemingly pure men of the Indies (East or West) who might serve as moral exemplars for sinful Europeans, so we are tempted to contemplate alien inquirers who surpass us in scientific wisdom and might assist us in overcoming our cognitive deficiencies. The idea is appealing, but it is also, alas, very unrealistic.

Still, whether it be androids produced in the laboratory or alien intelligences ("little green men") produced by nature on distant planets, the *philosophical* problems are much the same. These fall into three groups: the theoretical, the moral, and the practical.

The theoretical issues principally relate to matters of *recognition*: what it takes to establish agents (natural vs. artificial) as fellow rational beings, and what sorts of projects are inherently universal in their being so. (The idea of a discordant logic or arithmetic seems bizarre, but that of different customs or policies is altogether natural.)

The moral issues are primarily two. (1) *Acknowledgment*: Is it actually fellow rational beings that we are dealing with or a group of creatures that only seem to be rational or that might be sub-rational but remain at a lower level of cognitive functioning? (2) *Obligation*: What are our duties to these intelligent beings as either their superiors or inferiors?

And as regards the practical issues there again are primarily two. (1) *Communication*: How, if they indeed are sufficiently intelligent, can we possibly communicate with them? And (2) *coexistence*: How are we to achieve a modus operandi that enables us to live with each other peacefully and constructively?

In philosophy clarity can be helpfully facilitated by contrast with other alternatives—be it in reality or in hypothesis. Here too one learns much about one's own locale by traveling abroad to experience that of others.

RELATED ANECDOTES

3. Xenophanes's Animal Theologians   15
32. The Valladolid Debate   97
74. Wells's Neomen   210
96. Putnam's Twin Earth   268

FURTHER READING

Dick, Steven J. *Life on Other Worlds: The Twentieth-Century Extraterrestrial Life Debate.* Cambridge: Cambridge University Press, 2001.

Huygens, Christiaan. *Cosmotheoros: The Celestial Worlds Discovered—New Conjectures Concerning the Planetary Worlds, Their Inhabitants and Productions.* London: F. Cass, 1968.

Regis, E., ed. *Extraterrestrials.* Cambridge: Cambridge University Press, 1985.

43

LOCKE'S LOCKED ROOM

THEORETICIANS WHO DELIBERATE ABOUT freedom of the will often have it that an action is done freely and voluntarily only if the agent could have done otherwise. But this idea is undone by a clever counterexample already offered many years ago by John Locke (1632–1704). His account ran as follows:

> Suppose a man be carried, whilst fast asleep, into a room where there is a person he longs to see and speak with; and be there locked fast in, beyond his power to get out: he awakes, and is glad to find himself in so desirable company, which he stays willingly in, i.e., prefers his stay to going away. I ask, is not this stay voluntary? I think nobody will doubt it: and yet, being locked fast in, it is evident he is not at liberty not to stay, he has not freedom to be gone. So that liberty is not an idea belonging to volition, or preferring; but to the person having the power of doing, or forbearing to do, according as the mind shall choose or direct. Our idea of liberty reaches as far as that power, and no farther. For wherever restraint comes to check that power, or compulsion takes away that indifference of

ability to act, or to forbear acting, there liberty, and our notion of it, presently ceases.[1]

The salient point, of course, is that while the agent who remains in place under these postulated circumstances does so deliberately and voluntarily, so that his *act* of staying seemingly cannot but be accounted *free*, nevertheless he is not in the circumstance a *free agent* in Locke's sense of having "the power of doing, or forbearing to do, according as the mind shall choose or direct." So while that agent's act of staying is indeed free, nevertheless, paradoxical as this may sound, he is not in this instance a free agent.

The person who acts freely does what is in line with his or her naturally formed wishes rooted in the sort of person he or she is. Accordingly, even a wholly voluntary act is not free when done solely because the agent has been brainwashed into some unauthentic motivation for it by external manipulation. However, the fact that people are the sorts of persons they are through the course of nature's machinations rather than by personal choices is not the sort of "external" constraint that stands in the way of their freedom.

Freedom of the will and of action is an idea of great conceptual complexity, and people who eagerly rush to affirm or deny the existence of it are generally not prepared to take on the requisite preliminary labor of spelling out in exact detail just what this "it" is. In most of the vast literature on the topic—pro and con alike—one looks in vain for a detailed characterization of just exactly what would have to be the case for volitional freedom to exist. Like time, free will is one of those convoluted conceptions where it is all too tempting to think erroneously that one knows what one is actually talking about.

RELATED ANECDOTE

FURTHER READING

Locke, John. *An Essay Concerning Human Understanding*. London: T. Barret, 1960.
Rescher, Nicholas. *Free Will: A Critical Reappraisal*. New Brunswick: Transaction, 2009.

---

1. John Locke, *An Essay Concerning Human Understanding* (London: T. Barret, 1960), book 2, chap. 21, sect. 8.

44

LEIBNIZ'S TEXTUAL LIMIT

IN 1693 THE GERMAN philosopher, mathematician, and polymath G. W. Leibniz (1646–1716) launched into a series of studies of issues of eternal recurrence with a draft that was submitted to the Académie des Sciences in Paris and sent to its president, the abbé Bignon. Pursued under the heading of "palingenesis" or *apokatastasis*,[1] these studies afford an instructive insight into Leibniz's view of the human condition with regard to the limits of our knowledge.[2]

---

1. This term goes back to Plato's idea of a great "cosmic year" for the positional recurrence of the heavenly bodies and figures in the pseudo-Platonic dialogue *Axiochus* (370B). The term is also biblical, occurring at Acts 3:21. In its later, theological sense, *apokatastasis* relates to Origen's doctrine of the ultimate restoration of all men to friendship with God (a teaching sharply opposed by St. Augustine and ultimately declared anathema at the Council of Constantinople in 543).

2. Leibniz's tract *Apokatastaseōs pantōn* was originally published (and translated) by Max W. Ettlinger as an appendix to *Leibniz als Geschichtsphilosoph* (Munich: Koesel and Puslet, 1921). For an ampler treatment, see G. W. Leibniz, *De l'horizon de la doctrine humaine*, ed. Michel Fichant (Paris: Vrin, 1991). This work assembles the relevant texts and provides valuable explanatory and bibliographic material. See also Philip Beeley, "Leibniz on the Limits of Human Knowledge," *Leibniz Review* 13 (December 2003): 93–97.

Leibniz saw it as a key aspect of intelligent beings that they are symbol users, and that their propositional knowledge of matters of fact (in contrast to performatory, how-to knowledge) is unavoidably mediated by language. Whatever we factually know is—or can be—put into words. And in principle what is put into words can be put into print. This circumstance reflects—and imposes—certain crucial limitations. As Leibniz put it: "So since all human knowledge can be expressed by letters of the alphabet, one can say that one who understands the correct use of the alphabet perfectly knows everything. It follows that it would be possible to compute the number of truths accessible to us, and thereby determine the size of a work that could contain all possible human knowledge."[3]

Since any alphabet devisable by man will have only a limited number of letters (Leibniz here supposes 24), it transpires that even if we allow a word to become very long indeed (Leibniz supposes 32 letters) there will be only a limited number of words that can possibly be formed (namely, 24^{32}). And so if we suppose a maximum to the number of words that an intelligible statement can contain (say 100) then there will be a limit to the number of potential "statements" that can possibly be made, namely, $100 \exp (24^{32})$. Even with an array of basic symbols different from those of the Latin alphabet, the situation is changed in detail but not in structure. And this remains the case of the symbols at work at those of mathematics, where Descartes's translation of geometrically pictorial propositions into algebraically articulated form stood before Leibniz's mind, to say nothing of his own project of a universal language and a formal calculus of reasoning (*calculus ratiocinator*).

With an alphabet of 24 letters, there are 24^n words of exactly n letters. Accordingly, the total number of "words" with up to (and including) n letters will be, $24 + 24^2 + 24^3 + \ldots + 24^n$. Now a language whose average sentence is W words long and that has w words at its disposal will have some w^W available sentence-candidates. Most of this astronomical number of such symbolic agglomerations will of course be meaningless—and most of the remainder false. But this does not alter the salient and fundamental

---

3. Louis Couturat, *Opuscules et fragments inédits de Leibniz* (Paris: Alcan, 1903), 532. For further relevant detail, see Couturat's *La Logique de Leibniz* (Paris: Alcan, 1901).

fact that on the combinatorial approach projected by Leibniz, the number of possible books will be finite—albeit very large. Thus let it be—for example—that a book has 1,000 pages of 100 lines each of which has 100 letters. Then such a megabook will have room for 10^7 letters. With 24 possibilities for each of them, there will be at best 24 exp (10^7) possible books. No doubt it would take a vast amount of room to accommodate a library of this size, though. But it would clearly not require a space of Euclidean infinitude.[4]

Accordingly, Leibniz arrived at the striking conclusion that as long as people manage their thinking in language—broadly understood to encompass diverse symbolic devices—the facts that they possibly can know, while enormously large, are yet nevertheless bound to be limited in number. And considering that reality is of an unlimited complexity, this means that our language—and thereby our knowledge—is destined to be incomplete and imperfect.

RELATED ANECDOTES

70. Lasswitz's Library   **200**
75. Borel's Monkeys   **212**

FURTHER READING

Beeley, Philip. "Leibniz on the Limits of Human Knowledge." *Leibniz Review* 13 (December 2003): 93–97.
Borges, J. L. "The Total Library." *Selected Non-Fictions*. London: Penguin, 1999.
Leibniz, G. W. *De l'horizon de la doctrine humaine*. Edited by Michel Fichant. Paris: Vrin, 1991.

---

4.   The number of grains of sand in the world—which Archimedes had put at 10^{50}—is very small potatoes in comparison. The *Sand-Reckoner* of Archimedes, the grandfather of all studies of large numbers, introduces the idea of successively large ordains of magnitude via the relationship $e_n = 10^{8n}$. Archimedes sees the diameter of the sphere of the fixed stars no greater than 10^{10} stadia and, on this basis, states that the cosmos would be filled by 1000 $e_7 = 10^{50}$ grains of sand. See T. L. Heath, *The Works of Archimedes* (Cambridge: Cambridge University Press, 1897).

45

LEIBNIZ'S WINDMILL

THE QUESTION OF HOW—if at all—the human psyche is to be accounted for in terms of material nature's physical operations has long figured on philosophy's agenda. The issue became particularly critical in the wake of René Descartes's dualistic division of existence into disjoint sectors of mental and material being. In this context, Leibniz addressed the issue in one of the most oft-quoted passages of his classic *Monadology*:

> *Perception* and what depends upon it is *inexplicable on mechanical principles*, that is, by figures and motions. In imagining that there is a machine whose construction would enable it to think, to sense, and to have perception, one could conceive it enlarged while retaining the same proportions, so that one could enter into it, just like into a windmill. Supposing this, one should, when visiting within it, find only parts pushing one another, and never anything by which to explain a perception. Thus it is in the simple substance, and not in the composite or in the machine, that one must look for perception.[1]

---

1. G. W. Leibniz, *G. W. Leibniz's* Monadology: *An Edition for Students*, ed. Nicholas Rescher (Pittsburgh: University of Pittsburgh Press, 1991), sect. 17.

This passage is widely cited as a *proof text* for Leibniz's insistence on the explanatory irreducibility of mental to physical proceedings, and thereby as demonstrating his commitment to idealism. However, Leibniz qualified this exposition by moving from the macro level of man's experiential place in the world to the micro level of physical nature's ultimate constitution in subliminal reality:

> Each organized body of a living being is a kind of divine machine or natural automaton, which infinitely surpasses all artificial automata. For a machine constructed by man's art is not a machine in each of its parts. For example, the tooth of a brass wheel has parts or fragments which, for us, are no longer artificial things, and no longer have any marks to indicate the machine for whose use the wheel was intended. But natural machines, that is, living bodies, are still machines in their least parts, to infinity. That is the difference between nature and art, that is, between divine art and our art.[2]

As Leibniz saw it, the difference between minds and machines as we know them is one of infinite degree—and thereby effectively one of a kind.

> The moderns lack sufficiently grand ideas of the majesty of nature. They think that the difference between natural machines and ours is only the difference between great and small. . . . I believe that this conception does not give us a sufficiently just or worthy idea of nature, and that my system alone allows us to understand the true and immense distance between the least productions and mechanisms of divine wisdom and the greatest masterpieces that derive from the craft of a limited mind. For this difference is not just a difference of degree, but a difference of kind. We must then know that the machines of nature have a truly infinite number of organs, and are so well supplied and so resistant to all accidents that it is not possible to destroy them.[3]

So with Leibniz, as with most present-day natural scientists, the world of our experience is the natural product of the operations of

---

2. G. W. Leibniz, *G. W. Leibniz's* Monadology, sect. 65.

3. G. W. Leibniz, "New System of Nature" (1695), in *G. W. Leibniz: Philosophical Essays*, ed. and trans. Roger Ariew and Daniel Garber (Indianapolis: Hackett, 1989), 139.

an underlying manifold of unimaginably small subexperiential units of natural reality. With Leibniz, however, this ultimate level of existence consisted of minute size—more punctiform than even the micro "strings" of contemporary physics—units of natural operations of these subatomic "monads" (as he called them) produce all of the phenomena of "our world," thought and mental activity included.

On such a view, matter does not produce mind and mind certainly does not produce matter. Instead, both alike issue from the machinations of something more fundamental than either, something that is neither material nor mental in its own nature. It is indescribable in the terminology of our familiar experience but able, in the course of its operations, to function causally so as to bring us and our experience into being, even as letters of the alphabet on which the idea of meaning has no bearing can so function in suitable contexts as to engender words and sentences and thereby become meaningful. (A metaphysics of this sort, called "neutral monism," was revived in the early twentieth century by the English philosophers A. N. Whitehead and Bertrand Russell.)

Of course the difficulty of any such theory—unavoidable and perhaps inseparable as well—is to fill in the detail showing exactly how we are to get here from there. This set is a challenge that defeated the Greek Atomists in antiquity, Leibniz in the seventeenth century, and Russell and Whitehead in the twentieth century. And the ever-growing disconnection between subatomic microphysics and our phenomenal experience does not afford a promising prospect in this regard.

RELATED ANECDOTES

FURTHER READING

Leibniz, G. W. G. W. Leibniz's Monadology: An Edition for Students. Edited and translated by Nicholas Rescher. Pittsburgh: University of Pittsburgh Press, 1991.

Russell, Bertrand. The Analysis of Matter. London: Allen and Unwin, 1954.

Whitehead, A. N. Process and Reality. Cambridge: Cambridge University Press, 1929.

46

LEIBNIZ'S MYTHIC GODDESS

LEIBNIZ NOTORIOUSLY TAUGHT THAT this is the best of possible worlds. To be sure, he acknowledged its numerous negative and unfortunate occurrences and conceded that it is not perfect. But he held that no other realizable possibility will, on balance, be superior to it. In this context he sketched in his magnum opus, the *Theodicy*, the myth of Theodonis to whom, in a dream, a goddess reveals the book of fate describing the entire manifold of possibilities from among which Jupiter chose the best for actualization. And when the question arose why there exists a Sextus, who is both cause and victim of much suffering, the goddess responded:

> You see that my father, Jupiter, did not make Sextus wicked; he was so from all eternity, he was so always and freely. My father only granted him the existence which his wisdom could not refuse to the world where he is included: he made him pass from the region of the possible to that of the actual beings. The crime of Sextus serves for great things: it renders Rome free; thence will arise a great empire, which will show

noble examples to mankind. But that is nothing in comparison with the worth of this whole world, at whose beauty you will marvel.[1]

And so as Leibniz saw it, the world's very real negativities are outweighed—on the whole!—by sufficiently weighty compensating positivities.

In his novella *Candide*, Voltaire (1694–1778) envisioned a Leibniz stand-in, the smug Dr. Pangloss, who accompanies the naive young scholar Candide across a journey of many disasters, constantly voicing a facile optimism in the face of misfortune. Ultimately, Candide cries out: "But if this is the best of possible worlds, what in heaven's name can the others be like?"

Voltaire thought that with this question his guided tour of disasters refuted not just his Leibniz simulacrum Pangloss but also Leibniz himself. However, the real Leibniz could—and effectively did—have a ready answer: "Even worse."

However the problem that remains—and did not fail to trouble Leibniz—is that of justice. For even should it be that in this world the good outweighs the bad and pleasure outweighs pain on balance, the fact remains that this affords little consolation to those particular individuals who suffer. Something above and beyond best-*possible* world argumentation would be required to address this problem.

RELATED ANECDOTES

27. King Alfonso's Boast   81
73. The Monkey's Paw   208
98. Vagrant Predicates   273

FURTHER READING

Leibniz, G. W. *Theodicy*. Edited by Austin Farrer. Translated by E. M. Huggard. New Haven: Yale University Press, 1952.

Passmore, John A. *The Perfectibility of Man*. London: Duckworth, 1972.

Voltaire. *Candide*. Edited and translated by Robert M. Adams. New York: W. W. Norton, 1966.

---

1. G. W. Leibniz, *Theodicy*, ed. Austin Farrer, trans. E. M. Huggard (New Haven: Yale University Press, 1952), 372–73 (sect. 416).

ALDRICH'S BOX
PARADOXES

THE ENGLISH LOGICIAN, THEOLOGIAN, architect, and polymath Henry Aldrich (1647–1710), who was vice chancellor of Oxford University in the early 1690s, was fond of puns and puzzles. In the field of logic he inaugurated the idea of box paradoxes with the following simple example:

> Every sentence written
> in this box is false.

The paradox is obvious here: If the sentence in the box is true, then it is false; but if it is false, then it is true.

In an attempt to avert the problem, the suggestion is sometimes made that the sentence in question is meaningless and thus neither true nor false. But at this point there emerged the dual box paradox:

(1)

> Every sentence written
> in box (2) is false.

(2)

> Every sentence written
> in box (1) is false.

Here again there is an obvious logical conflict. But now it is difficult to dismiss those claims as meaningless. After all, the sentence of box 1—that very selfsame and unaltered sentence—is entirely unproblematic when box 2 contains the sentence "Two plus two is four."

The best plan here would be to regard the sentences at issue not as fixed single units but as contextually variable. So just as "It is raining *here*" is indefinitely schematic subject to the contextual specification of "here" or "It is raining *now*" is indefinitely schematic subject to the contextual specification of "now," so those boxed sentences are seen as indefinitely schematic, becoming well defined only contextually, subject to the specification of that other box. On this approach, those verbal complexes at issue do not constitute actually meaningful sentences unless and until they are embodied in a definite context to provide content.

A larger lesson thus emerges here, namely, that language is an imperfect instrument, and sometimes making proper communicative sense of what is being conveyed calls for complications that at first just do not meet the eye. For a verbalization that on one occasion presents a perfectly meaningful claim can disintegrate into incomprehensibility in a different setting. Language, the indispensable instrument of our thinking, can sometimes prove to be a treacherous ally.[1]

RELATED ANECDOTES

FURTHER READING

Clark, Michael. *Paradoxes from A to Z*. London: Routledge, 2002.
Rescher, Nicholas. *Paradoxes*. Chicago: Open Court, 2001.
Sternfeld, Robert. *Frege's Logical Theory*. Carbondale: Southern Illinois University Press, 1966.

---

1.   Nicholas Rescher, *Paradoxes* (Chicago: Open Court, 2001), 209–13.

48

MANDEVILLE'S BEES

INITIALLY TRAINED IN MEDICINE, Sir Bernard Mandeville (1670–1733) revolutionized social theory when he published his "Fables of the Bees" in the early 1700s. His tale contrasted two hives, the denizen of the one, having all the usual civic virtues, being frugal, abstemious, and dedicated to modest simple living; while those of the other hive were wasteful, profligate, high-living squanderers, devoted to material goods and intent on "living it up." But considered from an economist's point of view the "good" hive was impoverished and struggling with poverty and underemployment, while the "bad" hive thrived with its excess-supportive activity. Personal profligacy evokes the economic productivity required for its support.

Mandeville summed up the moral of his fable in the following:

> Then leave complaints: fools only strive
> To make a great an honest hive....
> Without great vices, is a vain
> Eutopia seated in the brain.
> Fraud, luxury, and pride must live,
> While we the benefits receive....

Do we not owe the growth of wine
To the dry shabby crooked vine. . . .
So vice is beneficial found,
When it's by justice lopp'd and bound. . . .
Nay, where the people would be great,
'Tis necessary to the state. . . .
Bare virtue can't make nations live
In splendor; they, that would revive
A golden age, must be as free,
For vices as for honesty.[1]

Thus Mandeville's two hives presented a striking discrepancy between moral virtue and economic affluence, with personally corruptive disruptive consumption engendering societally productive employment.

From the economist's point of view the tension is simple to resolve: neither can there be only consumers nor yet only producers—either a group of the one must be motivated by a group of the other or (better yet) a coordination can be effected at the level of individuals. (Say by arranging for a productive youth to be followed by a luxurious retirement.) But this matter of social arrangements does not address the moral issues.

The salient consideration here is that of choice. Even as an individual has to select a direction for allocating his or her efforts—deciding what sort of life to try making for oneself—so a society must resolve the issue of what sort of social environment it wants to create for itself. Viewed in this light, Mandeville's bee fable is less of a paradox than an object lesson regarding priorities in the biblical conflict between God and Mammon.

RELATED ANECDOTES

---

1. Bernard Mandeville, *The Fable of the Bees, or Private Vices, Public Benefits*, ed. I. Primer (New York: Capricorn, 1962), 38.

FURTHER READING

Heilbronner, Robert. *The Worldly Philosophers.* New York: Simon and Schuster, 1953.

Mandeville, Bernard. *The Fable of the Bees, or Private Vices, Public Benefits.* Edited by I. Primer. New York: Capricorn, 1962.

49

HUME'S SELF-SEEKING

THE SCOTTISH PHILOSOPHER DAVID HUME (1711–1776) was a dedicated empiricist who taught that our knowledge of matters of objective fact cannot possibly reach beyond the limits of our experience. This stance impelled him into various sorts of skepticism. For, as he saw it, we experience various particular and specific items but never the abstract relations and connections that obtain among them—so that relatedness in all its forms is in trouble. We experience occurrences in the world but not connections among them, thereby plunging the very idea of causality into trouble. We experience particular occurrence but never general (let alone universal) ones—so that the idea of necessity is in trouble. And we experience our various doings but never *ourselves*—and so the very idea of a *self* is in trouble.

Hume emphasized this last point as follows, "When I enter most intimately into what I call *myself*, I always stumble on some particular perception or other, of heat or cold, light or shade, love or hatred, pain or pleasure. I never can catch *myself* at any time without a perception and never can observe any thing but the perception. When my perceptions are removed for any time as by sound sleep; so long am I insensible of *myself*, and may truly be said not to exist."[1] Hume held that, where mental activity is concerned, the human mind is always an agent that feels this and sees that and never a mere patient. And it would accordingly be wrong to see the mind as something susceptible to observation or detection. Indeed, for Hume, there is, in the final analysis, no such *thing* as "the mind." Accordingly, Hume set out on a course of reasoning that followed the pattern:

- Our knowledge of fact entered no further than what is determined in our experience.
- Our experiences are always itemic (particular) and never relational (connecting)

- Therefore no knowledge of connectivity is possible for us— be that connectivity external in "the world" or internal in thought.

But even when the validity of this mode of argumentation is granted, the question "Just what does it show?" remains open. One can construe it as per Hume—to demonstrate that the conclusion obtains. Or inversely, one might perhaps in denying this conclusion construe it as a refutation of that first premise, thereby throwing into question the very sort of empiricism that Hume so ardently espouses.

RELATED ANECDOTES

FURTHER READING

Church, Ralph W. *Hume's Theory of the Understanding.* Ithaca: Cornell University Press, 1935.
Hume, David. *A Treatise of Human Nature.* Oxford: Oxford University Press, 2000.

---

1. David Hume, *A Treatise of Human Nature* (Oxford: Oxford University Press, 2000), book 1, chap. 4, sect. 6.

50

HUME'S SHADE OF BLUE

DAVID HUME HELD THAT the only conceptions that could figure meaningfully in our thinking were those that were to be grounded in perceptions—in matters of factual cognition, the human intellect had nothing to work with save for what is inherent in the material that the human senses put at its disposal. Thus in his *Enquiry Concerning Human Understanding* he wrote: "We shall always find, that every [conceptualized] idea which we examine is copied from a similar [sensory] impression. Those who would assert, that this position is not universally true nor without exception, have only one, and at that an easy method of refuting it; by producing that idea, which, in their opinion, is not derived from this source."[1] And yet, ironically, two paragraphs later Hume concedes such a counter-instance.

> There is, however, one contradictory phenomenon, which may prove that it is not absolutely impossible for ideas to arise, independent of their correspondent impressions. Suppose,

---

1. David Hume, *Enquiry Concerning Human Understanding* (New York: Washington Square, 1963), sect. 2, "Of the Origin of Ideas."

therefore, a person to have enjoyed his sight for thirty years, and to have become perfectly acquainted with colours of all kinds, except one particular shade of blue, for instance, which it never has been his fortune to meet with. Let all the different shades of that colour, except that single one, be placed before him, descending gradually from the deepest to the lightest; it is plain, that he will perceive a blank, where that shade is wanting, and will be sensible, that there is a greater distance in that place between the contiguous colours than in any other. Now I ask, whether it be possible for him, from his own imagination, to supply this deficiency, and raise up to himself the idea of that particular shade, though it had never been conveyed to him by his senses? I believe there are few but will be of opinion that he can: And this may serve as a proof, that the simple ideas are not always, in every instance, derived from the correspondent impressions; though this instance is so singular, that it is scarcely worth our observing, and does not merit that for it alone we should alter our general maxim.

Cognitive theorists and Hume interpreters alike have puzzled over what to make of this situation.

One possible reading is that Hume regarded this as the exception that proves the rule: that his concession does no more than indicate that the mind can move beyond the senses only in trivially minute steps.

Another approach would be to see the example as indicating that there just are no absolutely hard-and-fast universalizations with respect to philosophically relevant issues—that in this field every rule has its exceptions.

And a third possibly would be to insist that, Hume to the contrary notwithstanding, empiricism is simply wrong because the mind has the power to extract *suggestions* from experience that outrun the actual *data* of experience.

And so, clearly, there are distinct possibilities of resolution—but as is always the case with such philosophical issues, none is cost free. Each available resolution involves some commitments that—ideally considered—one might just not be all that eager to undertake, with each possibility having its downside. It would seem that in philosophy, as in life, there is no such thing as a wholly free lunch.

RELATED ANECDOTES

FURTHER READING

Hume, David. *A Treatise of Human Nature*. New York: E. P. Dutton, 1911.

Hume, David. *Enquiry Concerning Human Understanding and Other Essays*. New York: Washington Square, 1963.

Noonan, Harold W. *Hume on Knowledge*. London: Routledge, 1999.

51

KANT'S THINGS IN THEMSELVES

AS THE GERMAN PHILOSOPHER and polymath Immanuel Kant (1724–1804) saw it, our sense-perceptive capacity—"sensibility" he called it—enables us to perceive the appearance of things under certain corresponding modes of apprehension. Our sensibility does not give us access to how things are in themselves but only to how things appear to beings equipped with our particular sort of sensory apparatus:

> Even if we could bring our perception to the highest degree of clearness, we should not thereby come any nearer to the constitution of objects in themselves. We should still know only our way of perceiving, that is, our ways of sensing ("sensibility"). We should, indeed know it completely, but always only under the conditions that are originally inherent in the perceiving subject. What the objects may be in themselves would never become known to us even through the most elaborate knowledge of that which is alone given us, namely, their appearance.[1]

---

1. Immanuel Kant, *Critique of Pure Reason*, A43–B60.

What things are like in and of themselves, apart from our modes of perception—what things actually are like, as distinct from how they appear to us—is at best a matter of conjecture.

As Kant saw it the difference between "I (or we) think matters to stand X-wise" and "Matters do in fact stand X-wise" is insuperable: there just is no way of crossing the barrier between them. We must accordingly draw a distinction between the world of observational experience and reality itself—a distinction that we cannot implement in detail because we cannot exit from the former domain to detail its difference from the latter. We realize *that* there is a difference between reality and appearance, but we cannot say in detail *what* that difference is. Accordingly, Kant held that we simply cannot get beyond how things appear—how they present themselves to us. He believed that the instruction "Tell me what things are actually like as distinct from how they present themselves in experience" makes an inherently unmeetable demand.

The lesson that emerges here is effectively this: the only distinction between the *mere* or *seeming* surface appearance of things and their *authentic* appearance we can realistically draw is entirely intra-experiential and thus subject to the quality controls of careful inspection and cogent systematization.

RELATED ANECDOTES

FURTHER READING

Ewing, A. C. *A Short Commentary on Kant's Critique of Pure Reason.* Chicago: University of Chicago Press, 1938.

Kant, Immanuel. *Critique of Pure Reason.* Edited and translated by Marcus Weigelt. New York: Penguin, 2008.

Kuehn, Manfred. *Kant: A Biography.* Cambridge: Cambridge University Press, 2001.

52

KANT'S ERRAND BOY

IN HIS CLASSIC MONOGRAPH on *The Foundations of the Metaphysics of Morals*, Immanuel Kant drew the subtle but important contrast between acting morally on the one hand and merely doing what morality requires on the other. His line of reasoning ran as follows:

> It is easily decided whether an action in accord with duty is performed from duty or for some selfish purpose. It is far more difficult to note this difference when the action is in accordance with duty and, in addition, the subject has a direct inclination to do it. For example, it is in fact in accordance with duty that a dealer should not overcharge an inexperienced customer, and wherever there is much business the prudent merchant does not do so, having a fixed price for everyone, so that a child may buy of him as cheaply as any other. Thus the customer is honestly served. But this is far from sufficient to justify the belief that the merchant has behaved in this way from duty and principles of honesty.[1]

---

1. Immanuel Kant, *Foundations of the Metaphysics of Morals*, trans. L. W. Beck (New York: Bobbs-Merrill, 1959), sect. 1, 13.

To enjoy the reputation of being someone who treats people courteously and fairly is worth its weight in gold to any merchant or tradesman. And our merchant was thus well advised to treat that errand-boy with kindness and honesty. Here morality has prudence on its side. But—so Kant now goes on to insist—the matter goes much further. The agent who does the morally appropriate thing *only* because it is prudently self-advantageous—avoiding the loss of custom in our merchant case—is not really being moral at all.

The question of motivation is crucial here: acting rightly is not enough. For moral credit to result one must do the right thing for *the right reason*: because it is right rather than for the morally vitiating construction that it is going to be advantageous.

And here Kant's view of the matter was clearly on target. Doing the right things with selfish let alone malign intentions and doing the wrong thing with "the best of intentions" both alike represent morally flawed modes of behavior.[2] Moral credit—approbation and laudation—is in order only where the right thing is done for the right reason.

RELATED ANECDOTES

FURTHER READING

Kuehn, Manfred. *Kant: A Biography.* Cambridge: Cambridge University Press, 2001.
Stevens, Rex Patrick. *Kant on Moral Practice.* Macon: Mercer University Press, 1981.
Wood, Allen W. *Kantian Ethics.* Cambridge: Cambridge University Press, 2008.

---

2. People argue about what is the worse, but this does not interest Kant: his concern is with what is morally appropriate; the essence of comparative degree of inappropriateness remains outside this line of inquiry.

53

KANT'S PEACEFUL VISION

IN 1795 KANT PUBLISHED his much-discussed essay "Toward Permanent Peace" with the firm of his Königsberg friend Friedrich Nicolovius. In it he wrote: "If it is a duty to realize the condition of public right, even if only in approximation by unending progress, and if there is also a well-founded hope of this, then the perpetual peace that follows upon what have till now been falsely called peace treaties (strictly speaking, truces) is no empty idea but a task that, gradually solved, comes steadily closer to its goal (since the times during which equal progress takes place will, we hope, become always shorter)."[1] It was Kant's central thesis that the moral principles that govern the relations among individuals should also govern those among states: "The theoretical proposition that morality is superior to politics rises infinitely above all objections and is in fact the indispensable condition of all [appropriate conducted] politics." Kant's position was an intriguing combination of utopianism and realism as he saw it: perfection is unachievable in an imperfect

---

1. Immanuel Kant, *Practical Philosophy*, ed. M. J. Gregor (Cambridge: Cambridge University Press, 1996), 351.

world, but progress—ongoing improvement—is something that can be realized and should be striven for.

Those who have envisioned and advocated perpetual peace have generally done so for one of two reasons: *prudential utopianism* ("Wouldn't it be great if . . . ?") and *revealed religion* ("What sort of Christians are we when . . . ?"). Kant rejected both approaches. For him the cultivation of peace is a matter of *morality*—of abstaining from harm to those other intelligent beings who are our fellows in the community of man. As he saw it, social and political progress is something deeply bound up with personal morality because it is a moral obligation incumbent upon all to work toward its realization.

In Nazi Germany resistance to the regime—actual victims and enemies of the regime like Jews and Communists apart—came predominantly from three sources: religionists for whom behavioral standards were set not by the state but also by a higher source; aristocrats for whom the Nazi's brutish behavior was just not the sort of thing their sort of people countenance; and Kant-influenced people who accepted a duty to the cultivation of moral ideals. (There were, unfortunately, too few of them.)

Kant's vision of social and political progress in the world was a hallmark feature of the era we call the Enlightenment. Given a further ideological impetus in the age of Darwin, it suffered a drastic shock in the wake of World War I. That "war to end wars" did indeed engender the League of Nations, but this soon proved to be yet another object lesson for the difficulty of realizing Kant's peaceful vision in an all-too-imperfect world.

RELATED ANECDOTES

FURTHER READING

Kant, Immanuel *Practical Philosophy*. Edited by M. J. Gregor. Cambridge: Cambridge University Press, 1996.

Kuehn, Manfred. *Kant: A Biography*. Cambridge: Cambridge University Press, 2001.

54

KANT'S STARRY HEAVEN

ONE OF THE MOST quoted of Kant's notable passages comes from the concluding section of his *Critique of Practical Reason*: "Two things fill the mind with ever new and increasing admiration and awe, the oftener and more steadily we reflect on them: the starry heavens above me and the moral law within me." This passage reflects the eighteenth century's evolving preoccupation with the philosophy of artifice rather than nature and in particular with the aesthetic idea of the pleasing, the beautiful, and the more than beautifully sublime.

And it was this last conception—that of the sublime—that particularly fascinated Kant and engaged his interest. To facilitate entry into his thought on the subject, consider some passages amalgamated from his *Critique of the Power of Judgment*:

> The sublime is something whose very conception demonstrates a mental faculty that surpasses the reach of the senses, in that its apprehension embodies the idea of infinity. It is the product not of sensation but of reason, because reason inevitably enters in through its commitment to an absolute totality independent

of the sense, thereby inducing a feeling of the unattainability of its idea via the imagination. We deem sublime such things as the starry heavens, the vast oceans, man's free power of judgment, and the ideal it's known for—all viewed as idealizations that transcend any serious involvement, and reflective in a power of the mind to soar above the serious level through an involvement with rational principles.[1]

Like Plato, Kant saw reason (*logos*) as providing us with access to a reality above and beyond the commonplace realm of everyday life. And this Kantian Neo-Platonism was never more strongly in evidence than in his invocation of mind-projected ideas and ideals reflective of the power of reason to transcend the domain of sensuous apprehension.

RELATED ANECDOTES

FURTHER READING

Kant, Immanuel. *Critique of the Power of Judgment*. Translated by Paul Guyer and Eric Mathews. Cambridge: Cambridge University Press, 2000.
Kuehn, Manfred. *Kant: A Biography*. Cambridge: Cambridge University Press, 2001.
Wood, Allen W. *Kantian Ethics*. Cambridge: Cambridge University Press, 2008.

---

1. Immanuel Kant, *Critique of the Power of Judgment*, trans. Paul Guyer and Eric Mathews (Cambridge: Cambridge University Press, 2000), 5:153–54.

55

KANT'S REORIENTATION

AT THE OUTSET OF his *Prolegomena to Any Future Metaphysics* Kant made an observation that is all too rarely cited by later German philosophers: "There are scholarly men to whom the history of philosophy (both ancient and modern) is philosophy itself. . . . Such men must wait till those who endeavor to draw from the fountain of reason itself have completed their work; it will then be the turn of these scholars to inform the world of what has been done. Unfortunately, nothing can be said which, in their opinion, has not been said before, and truly the same prophecy applies to all future time."[1] The phenomenon to which Kant here averts has long characterized the philosophical scene. After all, philosophers have a choice: they can deliberate about a philosophical issue in and of itself or they can deliberate about the deliberations of others on the topic. And the latter is not only easier but also generally more appealing, given humans' natural pleasure in correcting the mistakes and shortcomings of others.

---

1. Immanuel Kant, *Prolegomena to Any Future Metaphysics*, trans. L. W. Beck (Indianapolis: Bobbs-Merrill, 1950), introduction.

The reality of it is that philosophical inquiry can be hard work. First, one needs to identify the predominantly significant and interesting issues. And then we find that every question admits of many possible answers—most of them of course wrong. Inquiry then becomes a matter of trying to find the right one—the needle in the haystack. Criticism, by contrast, is a matter of showing that this or that possible answer will not do. Where those possible answers are inherently clear, mutually exclusive, and collectively exhaustive then a process of elimination may well serve the interests of inquiry. But in philosophical matters these conditions are generally not fulfilled. The possibilities—and thereby the prospects of error—are unending. Eliminating some missteps need bring us no nearer to the truth of things. Those historical developments all too often afford trades to nowhere. And so, as Kant rightly stressed, the proper way to philosophize calls for addressing the issues themselves. Looking to what others have done with them will doubtless prove very helpful, but it does not accomplish the real job itself. As Kant saw it, philosophy needs to be reoriented from dwelling on what *has been* done to what *can be* done.

RELATED ANECDOTES

FURTHER READING

Despland, Michel. *Kant on History and Religion*. Montreal: McGill-Queen's University Press, 1973.
Kant, Immanuel. *Prolegomena to Any Future Metaphysics*. Translated by L. W. Beck. Indianapolis: Bobbs-Merrill, 1950.

56

CONDORCET'S PARADOX

THE IDEA OF MAJORITY rule forms part of the core of the democratic ethic. But unfortunately there are some serious obstacles to its implementation—and not just as a matter of practical procedure but as one of theoretical feasibility.

Suppose that three voters are asked to rank three options, with the following result:

	A	B	C
(1)	1st	2nd	3rd
(2)	3rd	1st	2nd
(3)	2nd	3rd	1st

No resolution available here will please everyone. But, even worse, since both A and C—a majority—prefer (3) to (2) it seems that the preferable ranking should be (3) > (2). But by exactly the same token regarding A and B we have (2) > (1). And again by the same token regarding C and A, we have (1) > (3). But the last two findings entail (3) > (3), which contradicts the first. Majority rule falls apart here. So runs the paradox of the Marquis de Condorcet (1743–1794), an ingenious French philosopher, mathematician, and political scientist who—along with many another talented individual—lost his life in the French Revolution.

Again, suppose a mini-community of three voters (A, B, C) who have to decide among three alternatives (say, which two of these candidates—a, b, c—are to be city counselors). Three propositions are put to a vote with the idea of letting a majority decide:

(1) Elect a
(2) Elect b
(3) Elect c

Our three voters vote for these three propositions as follows (with √ for pro, and X for con):

	A	B	C
(1)	X	√	√
(2)	√	X	√
(3)	√	√	X

Majority rule has clearly failed to eliminate anyone: every available alternative has majority approval.

Again consider the idea of a vote in our mini-community about building a bridge. There are three possible positions for its location, a, b, and c. And there are four propositions on the ballot:

(0) Don't build the bridge.
(1) Build the bridge but don't have it at a.
(2) Build the bridge but don't have it at b.
(3) Build the bridge but don't have it at c.

And let our voters once more cast the same ballots as before—apart from their unanimous rejection of alternative (0). Then while all voters unanimously favor building the bridge, the majority disfavors its location at any one of the three feasible sites. Though universally approved, the bridge is blocked by gridlock.

The point is that while, abstractly speaking, voting seems a good way of resolving public issues, it may well prove to be unavailing. Notwithstanding its attractions, electoral democracy is no political cure-all—even in theory, let alone in practice.

RELATED ANECDOTES

FURTHER READING

Arrow, Kenneth J. *Social Choice and Individual Values.* 2nd ed. New Haven: Yale University Press, 1963.

Black, Duncan. *The Theory of Committees and Elections.* Cambridge: Cambridge University Press, 1958.

Faquarson, Robin. *The Theory of Voting.* Oxford: Oxford University Press, 1969.

Howard, Nigel. *Paradoxes of Rationality.* Cambridge: MIT Press, 1971.

57

HEGEL'S REALITY

IN HIS *CRITIQUE OF PURE REASON*, Immanuel Kant had maintained that the human mind's natural impetus is to insist upon systematizing our knowledge of facts in a way that elucidates their interconnections. And he took this to mean that in the final analysis, the rational order of nature relates not to nature as such but rather to nature-as-we-understand-it, with the rational order we discern in the scheme of things thus rooted in the human mind's mode of operation. As he saw it: "Man is the lawgiver of nature." In Kant's wake, the German philosopher G. W. F. Hegel (1770–1831) took this mind-connective "idealistic" rationalism to its logical conclusion. As Hegel saw it, rationality is not just a characteristic feature of the human mind but also a force or power at work throughout nature. Cosmic history is the stage on which there develops not only life but also consciousness, self-consciousness, and self-directed agency (free will). As Hegel remarked at the outset of his *Philosophy of History*, "The history of the world is nothing other than the progress of the consciousness of freedom." And for Hegel, the process that drives this progress is a rational "dialectic." For even as rhetorical dialectic is an oscillating process of *contention/objection/response*, so the dialectical development of nature is an oscillating process of *innovation/obstacle-encounter/change.*

For Hegel the real is rational, not because rational beings can come to know it but because reality engenders creatures possessed of a rationality that for this very reason reflects reality's nature. And so, from Hegel's point of view, the Kantian thing-in-itself simply vanishes. There is no unbridgeable gap between the mind of rational inquiry and the reality of objective fact, because the reality of things is just exactly what the mind eventually comes to reveal in rational inquiry. With Hegel, reality and rationality harmonize because each of these potencies is at work in the construction of the other.

RELATED ANECDOTES

FURTHER READING

Inwood, Michael. *Hegel.* Oxford: Oxford University Press, 1985.
Taylor, Charles. *Hegel.* Cambridge: Cambridge University Press, 1979.

58

SCHOPENHAUER'S ANNOYANCE

ARTHUR SCHOPENHAUER (1788–1860) WAS an independently wealthy German philosopher whose massive study of "World as Will and Idea" was designed to realize the grand systemic aspirations of his place and time. While this work earned him enduring fame, he also achieved ongoing infamy through his negative view of women.

When a rooming house neighbor with whom he had quarreled with repeatedly over noise finally annoyed him beyond endurance, he gave her a push that caused her to fall. In doing so she injured her arm and thereupon sued him for damages. She was awarded a payment of fifteen thaler a quarter for twenty years. When she died after some time, Schopenhauer entered into his account book the Latin distich *"obit anus, abit onus"* ("The old woman dies, the burden departs"). His view of women in general was not much kinder.

His extensive writings include innumerable passages such as the following: "The fundamental flaws of the female character is that it has no sense of justice. This is principally due to the fact that

women are defective in the powers of reasoning and deliberation.
. . . They are dependent not upon strength, but upon craft."[1] What
Schopenhauer never properly acknowledged is the remarkably difficult and complex role that society has traditionally imposed upon
women. It involves an enormously challenging and demanding
life transit that begins with a youthful coquettehood, inducing the
errant male into a settled domesticity conducive to the secure continuation of the species. There then follows a period of maternal
maturity providing nurture during the childhood of her offspring.
And this is then followed by a period as family stabilizer among
the stresses of midlife crises, which is ultimately succeeded by functioning as a matriarchal consolidator of family values, providing
the dynastic glue that conjoins family members into a societal unit.
All this may perhaps characterize the ways of a now receding past,
but nevertheless it was a dominant pattern of society from classical
antiquity onward.

Since his philosophical writing adopted selflessness and self-
abnegation, whereas Schopenhauer himself led the life of a self-
centered curmudgeon in affluent comfort, the charge of hypocrisy
and inconsistency was made against him.

Schopenhauer replied that it sufficed for a philosopher to examine the human condition and determine the best form of life for
man: that he should also provide an example of it in his own proceedings was asking far too much.

Schopenhauer vividly illustrates the irony of the human condition where all too often the intellect acknowledges the advantage
of going where the will is unwilling to follow. And since this tension between intellect and will was the keystone of his philosophy,
Schopenhauer's proceedings did perhaps manage after all to provide
that example of living by one's doctrine.

In any case, Schopenhauer confronts us with the important
question of authenticity: of whether only those advisors can be re-
lied on who actually practice what is preached.

---

1. Arthur Schopenhauer, "On Women," *Arthur Schopenhauer: Essays and
Aphorisms*, ed. and trans. R. J. Hollingdale (New York: Penguin, 1970).

RELATED ANECDOTES

FURTHER READING

Copleston, Frederich. *Arthur Schopenhauer: Philosophies of Pessimism*. London: Search, 1975.

Mayer, Bryan. *The Philosophy of Schopenhauer*. Oxford: Oxford University Press, 1988.

Schopenhauer, Arthur. "On Women." *Arthur Schopenhauer: Essays and Aphorisms*. Edited and translated by R. J. Hollingdale. New York: Penguin, 1970.

THE RECENT
PAST,
1800–1900

59

J. S. MILL'S EPIPHANY

IN HIS CLASSIC *AUTOBIOGRAPHY*, the English philosopher John Stuart Mill (1806–1873) recounted an episode of his twentieth year that revolutionized his entire outlook for life.

Trained by his utilitarian father to see the aim of life as fostering the general welfare by promoting the greatest good of the greatest number, Mill now had second thoughts:

> It was in the autumn of 1826. I was in a dull state of nerves . . . the state, I should think, in which converts to Methodism usually are, then smitten by their first "conviction of sin." In this frame of mind it occurred to me to put the question directly to myself: "Suppose that all your objects in life were realized; that all the changes in institutions and opinions which you are looking forward to could be completely effected at this very instant: would this be a great joy and happiness to you?" And an irrepressible self-consciousness distinctly answered, "No!" At this my heart sank within me: the whole foundation

on which my life was constructed fell down. I seemed to have nothing left to live for.[1]

So Mill was now caught up in a tearing conflict of loyalties: What is it that is to be accepted as the primary aim and object of the good life, the promotion of the general welfare or the pursuit of personal happiness? Is pleasing others or pleasing oneself what ultimately matters? Is it our personal good or the general good that deserves primacy—should we be selfish or public spirited?

This conflict plunged Mill into a period of despondency from which only a reconciliation that would somehow harmonize these two conflicting desiderata could rescue him. Fortunately for Mill, he ultimately came to see his way clear on this:

> I never, indeed, wavered in the conviction that happiness is the test of all rules of conduct, and the end of life. But I now thought that this end was only to be attained by not making it the direct end. Those only are happy (I thought) who have their mind fixed on some object other than their own happiness; on the happiness of others, on the improvement of mankind, even on some art or pursuit, followed not as a means, but as itself an ideal end. Aiming thus at something else, they find happiness by the way. The enjoyments of life (such was now my theory) are sufficient to make it a pleasant thing, when they are taken *en passant*, without being made a principal object. Once make them so, and they are immediately felt to be insufficient. They will not bear a scrutinizing examination. Ask yourself whether you are happy, and you cease to be so. The only chance is to treat, not happiness, but something external to it, as the purpose of life.[2]

On this basis Mill found resolution for his frustrating conflict of loyalties, with altruistic benevolence and public-spirited behavior seen as itself affording a means to greater personal happiness.

For the medievals, making one's peace with God was the prime objective of a properly conducted life; for the moderns making

---

1. J. S. Mill, *Autobiography*, ed. J. M. Robson (New York: Penguin, 1989), chap. 5, "A Crisis in My Mental History."

2. Mill, *Autobiography*, "A Crisis in My Mental History."

one's peace with oneself has seemingly become the primary objective, carrying in its wake a dedication to the pursuit of happiness. But as Mill came to realize, care for others can and should form an integral part of this pursuit.

RELATED ANECDOTES

34. Dr. Faustus's Bargain   103
64. The Lady or the Tiger   184
93. Simon's Satisficing   260

FURTHER READING

McCabe, Herbert. *The Good Life: Ethics and the Pursuit of Happiness.* London and New York: Continuum, 2005.

Mill, J. S. *Autobiography.* Edited by J. M. Robson. New York: Penguin, 1989.

Swanton, Christine. *Virtue Ethics: A Pluralistic View.* Oxford: Oxford University Press, 2003.

60

DARWIN'S APE

THE THEORY OF EVOLUTION is inseparably bound up with the investigations and writings of the English naturalist Charles Darwin (1809–1882). His work represents one of the great scientific revolutions that transformed the tenor of the Western world's philosophical and intellectual culture. Darwin's overall position is set out in lucidly transparent prose:

> Thus we can understand how it has come to pass that man and all other vertebrate animals have been constructed on the same general model, why they pass through the same early stages of development, and why they retain certain rudiments in common. Consequently we ought frankly to admit their community of descent. . . . It is only our natural prejudice, and that arrogance which made our forefathers declare that they were descended from demi-gods, which leads us to demur to this conclusion. But the time will before long come, when it will be thought wonderful that naturalists, who were well acquainted with the comparative structure and development of man, and other mammals, should have believed that each was the work of a separate act of creation. . . .

Some of the most distinctive characters of man have in all probability been acquired, whether directly or more commonly indirectly through natural selection. . . .

The difference in mind between man and the higher animals, great as it is, certainly is one of degree and not of kind. We have seen that the senses and intuitions, the various emotions and faculties, . . . of which man boasts, may be found in an incipient, or over some time in a well-developed condition, in the lower animals.[1]

The history of thought has produced a series of major shocks to Western humankind's pretensions to a special status. The Copernican Revolution and the rise of modern astronomy expelled us from the special place at the center of the cosmos that Greek science had envisioned for us. The Age of Discovery saw European civilization demoted from its previously assured dominance of the terrestrial scene. The theory of evolution, with its absorption of humans into the overall developmental process of organic development, unraveled our claims to a separate and unique biological status. Neither astronomically, nor culturally, nor biologically were we humans now able to see ourselves as all that distinctive and special.

The only remaining prospect of yet another comparable blow to our pride would be the discovery of intelligent life on other planets, with its unraveling of our putative cosmic uniqueness as the sole bearers of rational, moral, and spiritual values. On this issue, only time will tell.

RELATED ANECDOTES

FURTHER READING

Coyne, Jerry A. *Why Evolution Is True*. New York: Viking, 2009.
Darwin, Charles. *The Descent of Man*. Revised ed. New York: A. L. Burt, 1874.
Pallen, Mark J. *The Rough Guide to Evolution*. New York: Rough Guides, 2009.

---

1. Charles Darwin, *The Descent of Man,* rev. ed. (New York: A. L. Burt, 1874), conclusion of chap. 1, conclusion of chap. 2, and start of chap. 3.

61

SAXE'S PUZZLING
ELEPHANT

THE AMERICAN POET AND journalist John Godfrey Saxe (1816–1887) was the nation's most notable humorist before Mark Twain. A Washington hostess regarded him as "deserving capital punishment for making people laugh themselves to death."[1] He earned lasting fame with his poem "The Blind Men and the Elephant," which tells the story of certain blind sages, those

> Six men of Indostan
> To learning much inclined
> Who went to see the elephant
> (Though all of them were blind).

One sage touched the elephant's "broad and sturdy side" and declared the beast to be "very like a wall." The second, who had felt its tusk, announced the elephant to resemble a spear. The third, who took the elephant's squirming trunk in his hands, compared it to a snake; while the fourth, who put his arm around the elephant's knee, was sure that the animal resembled a tree. A flapping ear con-

---

1.   Sara A. Pryor, *Reminiscence of Peace and War* (New York: Macmillan, 1929), 70.

vinced another that the elephant had the form of a fan; while the sixth blind man thought that it had the form of a rope, since he had taken hold of the tail.

> And so these men of Indostan,
> Disputed loud and long;
> Each in his own opinion
> Exceeding stiff and strong:
> Though each was partly in the right,
> And all were in the wrong.

Philosophers are all too prone to accuse their colleagues of leaping to large conclusions on small evidence. The danger of this failing—detected more readily in others than oneself—is among the instructive lessons of this philosophical poem.

To be sure, one might attempt to overcome this circumstance via the idea that different accounts—seemingly discordant philosophical doctrines—all quite correctly characterize the truths of different realms of one all-embracing reality. Viewed in this light, reality is complex and internally diversified, presenting different facets of itself to inquirers who approach it from different points of departure. And with such an approach, diverse philosophical systems could seem as describing reality variably because they describe it in different aspects or regards. *Everybody is right*—but only over a limited range. Every philosophical doctrine is true *more so*—in its own way. In principle, the various accounts can all be superimposed or superadded. Apparently diverse positions are viewed as so many facets of one all-embracing doctrine; they can all be conjoined by "but also." Such a multifaceted reality doctrine would combine the several apparently discordant alternatives in a way that gives to each a subordinate part in one overarching whole. Reconciliation between diverse doctrines can thus be effected additively through the conjoining formula "but furthermore in this regard," even as the elephant is spearlike in respect to his tusks and ropelike in respect to his tail.

William James's pluralism was of just this sort:

> There is nothing improbable in the supposition that an analysis of the world may yield a number of formulae, all consistent with

the facts. In physical science different formulae may explain the phenomena equally well—the one-fluid and the two-fluid theories of electricity, for example. Why may it not be so with the world? Why may there not be different points of view for surveying it, within each of which all data harmonize, and which the observer may therefore either choose between, or simply cumulate one upon another? A Beethoven string-quartet is truly, as someone has said, a scraping of horses' tails on cats' bowels, and may be exhaustively described in such terms; but the application of this description in no way precludes the simultaneous applicability of an entirely different mode of description.[2]

And so the sixty-four-dollar question arises: Are discordant philosophical views actually conflicting or are they mutually complementary—different components of one complex overall position?

It would, of course, be generous and irenic to take the view that everybody is right *in part*. But unfortunately this line does not look promising. For the reality of it is that philosophical views and positions are devised to conflict. Their very reasons for being of a given position in philosophy is to deny and contradict those discordant alternatives. And in the end we have little choice but to conjecture that the general reality of things is as our own limited experience of it shows it to be.

RELATED ANECDOTES

FURTHER READING

James, William. *The Will to Believe.* New York: Longmans Green, 1899.
James, William. *The Works of William James.* Edited by Frederick Henry Burkhardt. Cambridge: Harvard University Press, 1998.
Saxe, John Godfrey. *Poems.* Boston: Ticknor, Reed, and Fields, 1850.

---

2.   William James, "The Sentiment of Rationality," *The Will to Believe* (New York: Longmans Green, 1899), 76.

62

HERBERT SPENCER'S IMPATIENCE

IN HIS INTERESTING AND readable *Autobiography*, the English philosopher Herbert Spencer (1820–1903) narrated the following episode:

> [In my youth I encountered] a copy of a translation of Kant's *Critique of Pure Reason*, at that time, I believe, recently published. This I commenced reading, but did not go far. The doctrine that Time and Space are "nothing but" subjective forms—pertain exclusively to consciousness and have nothing beyond consciousness answering to them—I rejected at once and absolutely; and, having done so, went no further. . . . It has always been out of the question for me to go on reading a book the fundamental principles of which I entirely dissent from. Tacitly giving an author credit for consistency, I, without thinking much about the matter, take it for granted that if the fundamental principles are wrong the rest cannot be right; and thereupon cease reading—being, I suspect, rather glad of an excuse for doing so.[1]

---

1. Herbert Spencer, *Autobiography* (New York: Appleton, 1904), 1: 289.

Tempting though it might be, it would be rather unfair to counter this account by quoting the old bibliophile's quip that "A book is like a mirror: when a booby looks in, a genius cannot look out." For Spencer's response to Kant is neither unintelligible nor unjustified.

The issues that Kant's great work addresses and the ways and means by which he treats them are entirely outside of Spencer's range of familiarity and concern. He deserves no more reproach or reprehension for failing to grasp the significance of Kant's deliberations than someone would deserve condemnation for failing to understand a text written in Egyptian hieroglyphics. After all, Kant discusses the issues that concern him (and would also concern Spencer) within a range of concepts and perspectives that lies altogether outside of Spencer's conceptual horizon, and his reaction here is altogether natural and to be expected.

For the sake of comparison, consider the case of acupuncture. The Chinese adepts of this practice certainly have an explanation of its modus operandi. But the concepts and categories within which this explanation proceeds (via the causality flow of an internal bodily current called "the chi") is so far off the conceptual agenda of Western medicine and science as to be effectively unintelligible to us. One's thought cannot but move within the cognitive landscape of one's formative experience. Hamlet was doubtless right: "There are more things in heaven and earth, Horatio, than are dreamt of in your philosophy." It is not just that Aristotle did not think about quantum physics but that as matters stood he could not have. Understanding a discussion is not merely a matter of acumen but also requires having the body of experiences needed for entry into its concept-world.

RELATED ANECDOTES

FURTHER READING

Kant, Immanuel. *The Critique of Pure Reason*. Edited and translated by Marcus Weigelt. New York: Penguin, 2008.

James, William. *Pragmatism*. In *The Works of William James*. Edited by Frederick Henry Burkhardt. Cambridge: Harvard University Press, 1998.

Spencer, Herbert. *Autobiography*. 2 vols. New York: Appleton, 1904.

63

LORD KELVIN'S SUN

THE HISTORY OF SCIENCE affords some rather embarrassing situations of conflict and discord. For example, consider the following case: Adopting the stance of the physics of the 1890s, the eminent English physicist William Thomas, Lord Kelvin (1824–1907), regarded the sun as a thermodynamic burning process. Although this set the age of the solar system at a great many years, nevertheless looking to the geological strata led geologists and developmental biologists to require a timespan of at least ten times that length. Traditional Averroism had envisioned a conflict between two branches of thought: according to one (monotheistic religion), the universe was created and had a finite history; while according to another (Aristotelian philosophy), it was uncreated and had always existed. And now the same situation was seemingly replicated within natural science itself. For according to one of its branches (physics), the earth has a relatively short history; while according to others (geology and paleontology), its history had to be far longer.

This sort of doctrinal conflict within science is not all that rare. For quite a long time subatomic physicists divided into sectors that respectively saw photons as waves on the one side and as particles on the other. And to this day there is disconnection between relativity theorists who regard physical nature as fundamentally smooth and uniform and quantum theorists who see it as fundamentally granular and discrete. Just what is one to make of such a clash of scientific views?

In theory there are two basic possibilities.

One is the radical step of accepting a schizophrenic nature: to take in stride the idea that the world functions in one regard or context according to one set of laws and in another according to a set of laws incompatible with the former. To all viable appearance no one has actually advocated this sort of scientific Averroism.

The other possibility is not to charge the responsibility for incoherence to nature but rather to assume the responsibility for ourselves. This calls for taking the line that our present understanding is deficient, and that in the fullness of time further investigation will bring a consistency-restoring revision into view. In all the historic instances cited above this has in fact been the resolution adopted by those principally concerned. Our human commitment to intelligible order—both in ourselves and in nature's "rationality of the real"—simply goes too deep for any other course to be acceptable.

RELATED ANECDOTES

FURTHER READING

Burchfield, J. D. *Lord Kelvin and the Age of the Earth.* Chicago: University of Chicago Press, 1990.

King, A. G. *Kelvin the Man.* London: Hodder and Stoughton, 1925.

Sharlu, H. I. *Lord Kelvin: The Dynamic Victorian.* State College: Penn State University Press, 1979.

64

THE LADY OR THE TIGER

A PROVOCATIVE STORY TITLED "The Lady or the Tiger" was published in the *Century Magazine* in the 1870s by the American essayist Frank R. Stockton (1834–1902). In brief outline it ran as follows: Once upon a time, a cruel and despotic king had a beautiful daughter who was head over heels in love with a suitor knight whom the king regarded as altogether unsuitable. He sentenced the suitor to a trial by ordeal; requiring him to open one of two doors. Behind the one was a ferocious, starved tiger. Behind the other a beautiful countess, known to admire the suitor and now destined to be his bride if her door was chosen. The king's daughter discovered the secret of the doors, and as the knight was about to choose gave a signal to her suitor, who gladly accepted the guidance of her signal. But here the story stops, leaving the reader with the question: "What came out of the door—the lady or the tiger?"

Can our protagonist trust his inamorata, or might she be so possessively infatuated that she would rather see him dead than in the arms of a rival? And so as readers create their own ending to this story, they are enjoined to confront some large issues of philosophical orientation—among other things a view of human nature and in particular that of the female of the species. To all appearances, a good case can be made out for either alternative.

As philosophers address such issues, different value allegiances are bound to come to expression. Just as in this Stockton story, various alternatives for resolution arise and people will see them in a different light. And the manner in which this occurs is bound to reflect the experience of different individuals. But it is important to realize that this is not merely a matter of taste but also is—or should be—a rationally grounded reflection of the evidence afforded by people's different courses of experience with regard to how things work in the world.

RELATED ANECDOTES

FURTHER READING

Rescher, Nicholas. *The Strife of Systems.* Pittsburgh: University of Pittsburgh Press, 1985.

Zipes, Jack, ed. *Frank R. Stockton: Fairy Tales.* London: Penguin, 1990.

65

WILLIAM JAMES'S FREEDOM

THE HARVARD PSYCHOLOGIST AND philosopher William James (1842–1910) addressed the classic problem of freedom of the will on the basis of two premises:

1. As far as we can tell, free will is a possibility: no available evidence and no theoretical considerations rule out the possibility of free will.
2. Whenever *cognitive* considerations leave an issue undetermined, its resolution by a decision on the basis of "practical" (life-facilitating) considerations is a rationally acceptable and appropriate proceeding.

Accordingly, James purposed to reason as follows: "[For aught the cognitive considerations can venture the will is free and undetermined.] If, meanwhile, the will is undetermined, it would seem only that the belief in its indetermination should be voluntarily chosen from amongst other possible beliefs. *Freedom's first deed should be to affirm itself.*"[1] On this basis, James maintained free will as a self-

---

1. William James, *The Principles of Psychology* (London: Macmillan, 1890), 2: 573–79.

sustaining prospect: we have a free will because we can and do will ourselves to do so. And as he saw it, this stance is no more one of vitiating circularity than is our reason's insistence that only rationally cogent issue resolutions deserve to be seen as acceptable.

A free will, after all, is by definition one that functions unconstrained by other, external factors or forces. James held that our will can and should make this very fact manifest through an insistence to let nothing stand in the way of its self-affirmation. Humanity has so evolved in nature as to have a mind that demands rationality and sees itself as capable of acting under its guidance. Rationality will acknowledge no authority external to itself. And as James saw it, the situation regarding the will's freedom is essentially the same.

RELATED ANECDOTES

FURTHER READING

James, William. *The Principles of Psychology.* 2 vols. London: Macmillan, 1890.

James, William. *The Will to Believe.* New York: Longmans Green, 1899. Contains his essay on the "Dilemma of Determinism."

Kane, Robert, ed. *The Oxford Handbook on Free Will.* Oxford: Oxford University Press, 2002.

66

WILLIAM JAMES'S SQUIRREL

IN HIS CLASSIC 1896 lecture on "What Pragmatism Means," William James recounted the following episode:

> Some years ago, being with a camping party in the mountains, I returned from a solitary ramble to find everyone engaged in a ferocious metaphysical dispute. The *corpus* of the dispute was a squirrel—a live squirrel supposed to be clinging to one side of a tree-trunk; while over against the tree's opposite side a human being was imagined to stand. This human witness tries to get sight of the squirrel by moving rapidly round the tree, but no matter how fast he goes, the squirrel moves as fast in the opposite direction, and always keeps the tree between himself and the man, so that never a glimpse of him is caught. The resultant metaphysical problem now is this: *Does the man go round the squirrel or not?* He goes round the tree, sure enough, and the squirrel is on the tree; but does he go round the squirrel? In the unlimited leisure of the wilderness, discussion had been worn threadbare. Everyone had taken sides, and was obstinate; and the numbers on both sides were even.

James proposed to resolve the matter by the classic philosophical principle that "whenever you meet with a contradiction you must draw a distinction." For as he saw it, the issue

> depends on what you *practically mean* by 'going round' the squirrel. If you mean passing from the north of him to the east, then to the south, then to the west, and then to the north of him again obviously the man does go round him, for he occupies these successive positions. But if on the contrary you mean being first in front of him, then on the right of him, then behind him, then his left, and finally in front again, it is quite as obvious that the man fails to go round him, for by the compensating movements the squirrel makes, he keeps his belly turned towards the man all the time, and his back turned away. Make the distinction, and there is no occasion for any further dispute. You are both right and wrong according as you conceive the verb 'to go round' in one practical fashion or the other.[1]

When we adopt a certain distinction and thereby allow several different constructions for our terminology, this means that the theses formulated by this terminology can be viewed from different conceptual perspectives. And even as different physical perspectives will constrain differences in what we can appropriately claim to *see*, so differences in terminological perspectives will make for differences in what we can appropriately *claim*.

In this case, however, James's proposed solution of the dispute in question does not really quite work. For it will not do to give to "going around" the Jamesean interpretation of "being put in front of him, then on the right of him, then behind him, then on the left, and finally in front again." For just this can be accomplished by having the observer remain fixedly in place with the squirrel making a complete rotation in its place. And then of course there is simply no question of the observer's going around the squirrel.

All the same, two significant philosophical lessons are actually at stake here. The first is James's own, namely, that drawing distinctions affords an effective way of averting contradictions that would otherwise baffle us. And the second is that the language we use and

---

1. William James, *Pragmatism*, ed. Frederick Henry Burkhardt (Cambridge: Harvard University Press, 1979), lecture 2, "What Pragmatism Means."

the concepts it embodies will, once in place, impose limits on what we can appropriately affirm by their means. When we lay down rules of the game (so to speak), then those will impose limits on the moves we can justifiably make.

James's semantical pragmatism never had the impact among later theorists of meaning for which he had hoped. These theoreticians were mostly fixated upon issues of discourse and textuality, and for them the meaning of a statement was to be a matter of its evidentiation and of its consequences. James, however, had wanted to shift the issue from this textual concern to the practical and behavioral realms.[2] As he saw it, the key to meaning is action: the difference that accepting the statement as true or rejecting it as false would make in the realm of our behavior and conduct. The proof of the pudding of statement meaning has to lie in its eating—in what is done about it and not in the relation of statements to one another. But the linguistic turn of recent philosophy had the result that this language-transcending approach never got much of a run for its money.

RELATED ANECDOTES

FURTHER READING

Gale, Richard. *The Philosophy of William James*. Cambridge: Cambridge University Press, 1999.

James, William. *Pragmatism*. Edited by Frederick Henry Burkhardt. Cambridge: Harvard University Press, 1979.

Myers, Gerald E. *William James: His Life and Thought*. New Haven: Yale University Press, 1986.

---

2. In this regard James was influential not only for the American school of pragmatism but also for the Polish school of praxeology whose prime exponent was Tadeusz Kotarbiński (1886–1981).

67

KROPOTKIN'S
COOPERATORS

PETER KROPOTKIN (1842-1921) WAS an odd duck, to put it colloquially. Born a prince before the abolition of serfdom in Russia, he became a leading figure in that country's anarchist movement. His claim to philosophical fame, however, lies in his book *Mutual Aid: A Factor of Evolution* published in 1902 during his exile in England.

In the wake of Charles Darwin's landmark work on evolution by natural selection there arose a school of social Darwinists eager to apply the biological ideas of "survival of the fittest" in the social and political arena. They saw biological evolution by rational selection as replicated in the social arena, with the socioeconomic political elite achieving this role precisely because they were the best fitted for it. Against this view Kropotkin urged the following, very different perspective: Evolutionary survival has been the result not so much of a victory in conflict among individuals but rather of the benevolence of groups. For the survival of individuals does not hinge solely—or even primarily—on the personal qualities and characteristics of individuals as upon the originality of their environing groups for providing material aid through cooperation. Be it with human tribes or herds of elephants or colonies of ants, the survival of individuals is determined by the makeup and modus operandi of groups and the behavior of their members. The mutual aid and cooperative collaboration that members of a functioning social unit render to one another contribute to the opportunities for survival and reproduction of every member. Not rivalry, competition, and struggle but rather cooperation, collaboration, and mutual aid are to be seen as the key factors in their evolutionary development of species.

The early theorists who sought to find sociopolitical implications in Darwinian biology decided to emphasize the element of competition inherent in a "struggle for survival." Kropotkin's work managed to turn this around. He built up a strong case for his thesis that mutual aid constitutes a crucial factor in both biological and social evolution. And his emphasis on reciprocal support and collaboration breathed fresh air not just into biological study but also into the sociopolitical ideology of the day.

The idea that the individual was greatly advantaged by becoming the member of a mutually supportive group gave the themes of cooperation, collaboration, and mutual aid a place of prominence on the agenda of evolutionary theory. For the instrumentalities of collaboration—and above all good will and trust—are critical to the well-being of individuals who almost invariably depend on others for their own well-being and survival. And on this basis Kropotkin's approach provided for a more positive and far friendlier theory of man's place in society and in nature, as well as for a more constructive philosophical perspective on the human condition.

RELATED ANECDOTES

FURTHER READING

Axelrod, Robert. *The Evolution of Cooperation*. Revised ed. New York: Perseus, 2006.

Bowler, Peter J. *Evolution: The History of an Idea*. Berkeley: University of California Press, 1984.

Kropotkin, Peter. *Mutual Aid: A Factor of Evolution*. London: Freedom, 2009.

68

NIETZSCHE'S REVALUATION

IN CULTURAL HISTORY, EVERY china shop has its bull, and the German philosopher Friedrich Nietzsche (1844–1900) was eager to take on this role in philosophy. Historically, philosophers had always used reasoned argumentation as a method; Nietzsche proposed to abandon this in favor of bombast. Historically, philosophers had sought to induce a reluctant humankind into the paths of civility and virtue; Nietzsche thought us to be insufficiently dedicated to selfishness and power. Historically, philosophers generally had good things to say for morality; Nietzsche took a different line. In his *Ecce Homo* Nietzsche began the section "Daybreak" by saying "My campaign against morality begins with this book." And he proceeded to enunciate his programmatic manifesto:

> The start of a new day, indeed of a whole series, a whole world of new days. In a *revaluation of all moral values*, in an escape from all moral values, in an affirmation and trust in weighing that has been forbidden, despised, cursed, until now. This *affirmative* book saves its light, its love, its tenderness for bad things alone, it gives them back their "soul," a good conscience, the high right and

privilege to exist. Morality is not attacked, it just does not come into consideration any more.[1]

Nietzsche dreamt of being to the old moral order what Robespierre had been to the old political order.

It must, however, be acknowledged that there was a method to Nietzsche's madness. For the history of European society and culture since the Age of Enlightenment had seen a slow but steady drift toward a democratic egalitarianism—a sociopolitical order where everyone counts (equally?!). And in its wake there also emerged an ever-stronger sociopolitical tendency to make the world safe—and even comfortable—for "the little people." Yet as Nietzsche (and eventually many others) saw it this sort of thing has its downside because:

- it downgrades the commitment to and pursuit of excellence and outstanding work in just about any area
- it discourages aspirations toward achievement beyond the ordinary
- it exalts mediocrity

Nietzsche saw the modern dedication to democratic egalitarianism as an obstacle blocking the way to a pursuit of the extraordinary and excellent.

To be sure, this view of things reflects the positive side of Nietzsche's worldview. Had he articulated it in a calmly reasoned way, it might well have won him more—and more respectable—supporters. But then he would not have been Nietzsche.

RELATED ANECDOTES

FURTHER READING

Kaufmann, Walter. *Nietzsche*. 4th ed. Princeton: Princeton University Press, 1974.
Tanner, Michael. *Nietzsche*. Oxford: Oxford University Press, 1994.

---

1. Friedrich Nietzsche, *Ecce Homo*, in *Nietzsche:* The Anti-Christ, Ecce Homo, Twilight of the Idols *and Other Writings*, ed. Aaron Ridley and Judith Norman (Cambridge: Cambridge University Press, 2005), 120–21.

69

NIETZSCHE'S LONG RUN

ESCHATOLOGY IS THE DOCTRINE of the long run—of how things will work themselves out in the end. In the history of philosophical speculation there have been three main theories on the subject—alterationism, progressivism, and recurrentism. They run roughly as follows:

> *Alterationism* is the doctrine of "ever more and different." Its principle is that of ongoing novelty—there will be ever new sorts of occurrences and the past affords no guidance to or prediction of the future.
>
> *Progressivism* is the doctrine of "ever more and better." Its principle is that of progress—that the new occurrences of the future will always improve in some significant respect and that the world's future will ongoingly prove to be better than its past.
>
> *Recurrentism* is the doctrine of "there is nothing new under the sun"—essentially the future does no more than to provide replays of the past.

An early version of the eternal recurrence idea was pervasive in antiquity since Babylonian times, whose present sages contemplated a vast cosmic conflagration (*ekpyrosis*) in which the world was destroyed (*apokalypsis*) only to be reborn anew, re-arising like the mythic Phoenix from its own ashes to repeat the earlier cycle. And the corresponding idea of all-comprehending cosmic circle, over which the world becomes dissolved and then starts again, has figured on the agenda of philosophy since the dawn of the subject.[1] In Greek antiquity such a conception of rebirth (*palingenesis*) played a key role in the physical theory of the Stoics who (somewhat dubiously) ascribed its origin to Heraclitus.[2]

The prime advocate of this position in modern philosophy was Friedrich Nietzsche who called himself "the teacher of the eternal recurrence," characterizing this as "the doctrine of the eternal recurrence, i.e., of the unconditional and infinitely repeated circular course of all things."[3] And in one of Heinrich Heine's books (which Nietzsche owned), there is a story whose protagonist declares:

> Time is infinite, but the things in time, the concrete bodies, are finite. They may indeed disperse into the smallest particles; but these particles, the atoms, have their determinate number, and the number of the configurations that, all of themselves, are formed out of them is also determinate. Now, however long a time may pass, according to the eternal laws governing the combinations of this eternal play of repetition, all configurations that have previously existed on this earth must yet meet, attract, repulse, kiss, and corrupt each other again. . . . And thus it will happen one day that a man will be born again, just like me.[4]

And this, in effect, is how Nietzsche himself saw the matter. He wrote that "The number of states, alterations, combinations, and developments of this [self-maintaining] force [in nature] is, to be

---

1. See John Burnet, *Early Greek Philosophy* (London: A. C. Black, 1892), 156–63, and more generally Ned Lukacher, *Time-Fetishes: The Secret History of Eternal Recurrence* (Durham: Duke University Press, 1998).

2. On Heraclitus's views, see Diogenes Laertius, *Lives of the Philosophers* (Chicago: H. Regnery, 1969), book 9, 9.

3. Friedrich Nietzsche, *Ecce Homo*, quoted in Walter Kaufmann, *Nietzsche: Philosopher, Psychologist, Antichrist* (San Francisco: Harper and Row, 1984), 317.

4. Quoted in Kaufmann, *Nietzsche*, 318.

sure, tremendously large and practically 'immeasurable,' but in any case also determinate and not infinite. . . . Consequently, the development of this very moment must be a repetition, and likewise the one that gave birth to it and the one that arises out of it and thus forward and backward further! *Everything has been there countless times inasmuch as the total state of all forces always recurs.*"[5]

But there are problems here, not only practical but also theoretical as well. For even very simple repetitive processes need not issue in cyclical recurrence. Consider three planets moving with uniform velocity in circular orbit around a common center.

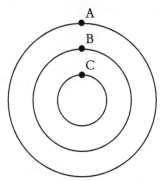

Let it be that A completes one orbit in $\sqrt{2}$ days, B one in 2 days, and C one in 1 day. Then B and C will recur to their indicted initial positions every N days whenever N is even. But at no time when N is even will A ever again be aligned with B and C in those positions. Notwithstanding the simple periodicities at issue, the indicted A-B-C configuration just cannot recur: never again will those three uniformly moving planets recover their initial alignment.[6]

The fact that there is going to be *some* "eternal recurrence" in the overall series does *not* mean that *any given* segment is going to

5. *Nietzsche's Werke,* Grossoktav ed. (Hamburg: Felix Meiner, 1986), 12: 51 (emphasis added). Nietzsche's argumentation would plausibly engender its intended conclusion only for a universe of finite variety and pure chance.

6. A more general argument to this conclusion was initially presented by Georg Simmel, *Schopenhauer und Nietzsche: Ein Vortragszyklus* (Leipzig: Duncker and Humblot, 1967), 250–51.

repeat.[7] *Repetition simply need not entail cyclic periodicity.* Even in a world of rather limited scope and complexity, as long as numerical measuring and not just successive counting is in prospect, there need be no repetition, let alone unending cyclicity. And much the same holds true with discourse as well, where there beckons the unending prospect of saying new things with the same old sounds.

The aficionados of eternal recurrence err in taking an overly restrictive view of the vast range of possibility.

RELATED ANECDOTES

FURTHER READING

Kaufmann, Walter. *Nietzsche*. 4th ed. Princeton: Princeton University Press, 1974.
Lukacher, Ned. *Time-Fetishes: The Secret History of Eternal Recurrence*. Durham: Duke University Press, 1998.
Rescher, Nicholas. *Studies in Quantitative Philosophizing*. Frankfurt: ONTOS, 2010.

---

7.   To be sure, in a series of finitely many states driven by *pure chance* any particular segment of *n* states is effectively certain to recur sooner or later. For a study of the relevant scientific issues, see Abel Rey, *Le retour éternel et la philosophie de la physique* (Paris: Flammarion, 1921).

70

LASSWITZ'S LIBRARY

THE GERMAN PHILOSOPHER Kurd Lasswitz (1848–1910) was also one of the founding fathers of science fiction writing. In his 1901 story of "The Universal Library" ("Universalbibliothek") he contemplated a total library of infinite scope, somewhat along the following lines: There is to be a special, elaborate symbolic "alphabet," variegated enough to serve for any conceivable language. Texts of every combinationally possible sort of expressible means of this alphabet—and thus everything expressible in any possible language—are to be gathered together in one infinitely vast library, a storehouse of everything sayable in matters of fact and of fiction. The generic idea that everything sayable (and thus any thinkable idea) is somehow encompassed in one vast alphabetic manifold and can in principle be recorded in a library of more than astronomical scope is virtually as old as the idea of libraries as such. Likely, it was already a glimmer in the mind of the librarians of ancient Alexandria, but in any case it was already contemplated by Leibniz, who provided the impetus for J. L. Borges's widely admired essay on "The Total Library" ("La bibliotheca total").

With Leibniz this idea of an infinite, all-encompassing textuality took a theological form, providing the basis for the conception of a "manifold of possibility" existing in the mind of God, a quasi-textual realm encompassing a complete description not only of this world but also of every possible world whatsoever. World orientation accordingly becomes a matter of selection, owing to the alternatives encompassed in such a marking of all available possibilities.

Of course among all those endless books detailing unendingly varying conceivable scenarios, there is bound to be one that details the actual world. This could be viewed in two very different perspectives. If it were fixed from the outset that this book holds the world's history, then it could be named *The Book of Fate* that lies at the core of the expression "It is written," which is dear to the fatalistic theorists of the East. If, on the other hand, it is seen as certifiably authentic only ex post facto as the world's history unfolds, then it could never be identified until that history itself has ended (and so perhaps never!).

It must be recognized, moreover, that a predetermination of the world's occurrences will not necessarily block the prospect of free agency. For what might be fated is exactly that a certain choice be made freely. There is nothing unfree about the will that spontaneously opts for the inevitable. (Think here again of Anecdote 43, Locke's Locked Room). Indeed just here lay Spinoza's vision of human freedom—as a matter of aligning our choices and actions with the world's inevitable actualities.

RELATED ANECDOTES

FURTHER READING

Beeley, Philip, ed. "Leibniz on the Limits of Human Knowledge." *Leibniz Review* 13 (December 2003): 93–97.

Borges, J. L. "The Total Library." *Selected Non-Fictions*. London: Penguin, 1999.

Leibniz, G. W. *De l'horizon de la doctrine humaine*. Edited by Michel Fichant. Paris: Vrin, 1991.

Lasswitz, Kurd. *Traumkristalle*. Not translated but an important source for Borges.

71

FREGE'S MORNING STAR

THE GERMAN MATHEMATICIAN AND logician Gottlob Frege (1848–1925) did much to make the basic ideas of mathematical discourse and reasoning clear and precise. One of his significant contributions related to the distinction between the *sense* and *reference* of discourse. Frege explains the idea as follows: "It is natural, now, to think of there being connected with a sign (name, combination of words, written mark), besides that which the sign denotes or designates, which may be called the *referent* [*Bedeutung*] of the sign, also what I should like to call the *sense* [*Sinn*] of the sign, wherein the mode of presentation is contained, . . . the referent of 'evening star' would be the same as that of 'morning star,' but not the sense."[1] And Frege proceeded to implement this distinction as follows:

> When we replace one word of the sentence by another having the same *referent* but a different *sense*, this can have no effect upon the *referent* of the sentence. Yet we can see that in such a case the thought changes; e.g., the thought in the sentence "The Morning

---

1. Gottlob Frege, *Gottlob Frege: Collected Papers*, ed. Brian McGuinness (Oxford: Blackwell, 1984), 158.

Star is a body illuminated by the Sun" differs from the sentence "The Evening Star is a body illuminated by the Sun." Anybody who did not know that the Evening Star is the Morning Star might hold the one thought to be true, the other false.[2]

But when one applies this idea of replacement invariance to the entire sentence itself, then the only thing that need remain the same when one true sentence is substantiated from another is the truth of that sentence. On this basis, Frege deemed the referent of sentences to be their status as simply true or false, despite their endless variation in regard to sense.

Frege's mode of interpretation, as well as his preparedness to follow logic where it leads—notwithstanding any conflict with our presystematic, everyday view of things—provided a guiding inspiration to one prominent mode of philosophizing in the twentieth century, that of the so-called analytic school.[3] Its adherents held that language is not just the arbiter of meaning in philosophy but that of doctrine as well. And so, as these theorists viewed the matter, philosophical problems must be investigated and resolved (or perhaps even dissolved) by close examination of the relevant machinery of discourse, with the properties of thought extracted from close attention to those of language.

RELATED ANECDOTES

FURTHER READING

Frege, Gottlob. *Gottlob Frege: Collected Papers.* Edited by Brian McGuinness. Oxford: Blackwell, 1984.

Frege, Gottlob. "On *Sinn* and *Bedeutung*." In *The Frege Reader*. Edited by Michael Beaney. Oxford: Blackwell, 1997.

Kenny, Anthony. *Frege: An Introduction to the Founder of Modern Analytic Philosophy.* London: Penguin, 1995.

---

2. Gottlob Frege, "On *Sinn* and *Bedeutung*," in *The Frege Reader*, ed. Michael Beaney (Oxford: Blackwell, 1997), 156.

3. On analytic philosophy, see Michael Dummett, *The Origins of Analytic Philosophy* (Cambridge: Harvard University Press, 1993); and John Passmore, *A Hundred Years of Philosophy* (New York: Basic, 1966).

72

DURKHEIM'S SUICIDES

THE FRENCH SOCIOLOGIST ÉMILE Durkheim (1858–1917) gave a new twist to the way in which statistical information shapes our understanding of humans' relationship to social affairs. It emerges from the tenor of his analysis of the statistics of suicides, which is conveyed by the following composite quotation:

> Every page of this book . . . [substantiates] the impression that the individual is dominated by a moral reality greater than himself: namely, collective reality. . . .
>
> The social suicide-rate can be explained only sociologically. At any given moment the moral constitution of society establishes the contingent of voluntary deaths. There is, therefore, for each people a collective force of a definite amount of energy, impelling men to self-destruction. The victim's acts which at first seem to express only his personal temperament are really the supplement and prolongation of a social condition which they express externally. . . . The social environment is fundamentally one of common ideas, beliefs, customs and tendencies. For them to impart themselves thus to individuals, they must somehow exist independently of individuals; and this approaches the solution

we suggested. For thus is implicitly acknowledged the existence of a collective inclination to suicide; from which individual inclinations are derived, and our whole problem is to know of what it consists and how it acts. . . .

The individuals making up a society change from year to year, yet the number of suicides is the same so long as the society itself does not change. The population of Paris renews itself very rapidly; yet the share of Paris in the total of French suicides remains practically the same. Although only a few years suffice to change completely the personnel of the army, the rate of military suicides varies only very slowly in a given nation. In all countries the evolution of collective life follows a given rhythm. . . . Collective tendencies have an existence of their own; they are forces as real as cosmic forces, though of another sort; they, likewise, affect the individual from without, though through other channels. . . . Since, therefore, moral acts such as suicide are reproduced not merely with an equal but with a greater uniformity, we must likewise admit that they depend on forces external to individuals. Only, since these forces must be of a moral order and since, except for individual men, there is no other moral order of existence in the world but society, they must be social. . . .

The productive cause of the phenomenon of the stability of suicide rates naturally escapes the observer of individuals only; for it lies outside individuals. To discover it, one must raise his point of view above individual suicides and perceive what gives them unity.[1]

The startling fact about suicides that deeply impressed Durkheim is what might be termed their *statistical stability*. Personally eccentric though a decision for self-annihilation may be, it nevertheless seems as though the finger of Fate taps the shoulders of just so many Frenchmen each year to make their contribution willy-nilly to an annual quota of self-murderers. The stability of such social statistics through constituting stable "rates" is in this case problematic in a way that goes beyond the mechanisms of demographic statistics.

---

1. Émile Durkheim, *Suicide: A Study in Sociology* (Glencoe: Free, 1951), 38, 299–302, 307–9, 324.

A society-pervasive causal mechanism seems to be at work to produce an overall result that cannot be derived from or reduced to individual characteristics or productivities. And of course much the same sort of thing happens in many regards: automobile collisions, murders, criminality, divorces, and so on. To be sure, in such matters one cannot tell in advance of the fact just who the victims will be: their identity is invisibly hidden away in a statistical fog. But the quantities at issue can be securely predicted in advance. One can confidentially say *that* a certain number of people will commit suicide (or murder, etc.) but of course cannot say *who*. The situation is much like that of a game of musical chairs—one can be sure *that* someone will remain unseated when the music stops, but one cannot possibly say *who* this will be. Even so, in dealing with societies, there is much information available by way of "the knowledge that" but far, far less by way of "the knowledge who." And even inert nature exhibits the same phenomenon with its baffling puzzle of the forces at work in or upon individuals to constrain a statistical regularity on the mass. (Thus plutonium 241 has a half-life of fourteen years, but what induces its individual atoms to fall into line so as to yield this outcome is a puzzle.)

Statistical fog plays an important role in human judgment. We know that some three hundred people will be killed in automobile accidents on a major holiday weekend in the United States. If it were known in advance who they were to be, there would be a drastic reaction—the whole road system might be shut down. (Think of the extent of reaction when someone is trapped in an underground shaft.) We tolerate the mayhem at issue only because the outcome is imponderable. And analogously, the stock market can function as is only because the price movements in the short-term future are hidden in the statistical fog.

And this situation is pervasive in human affairs, where specific predictions are generally impracticable. Modern societies can only manage their affairs on the basis of social statistics and the quantified analysis of the relationships that they reveal. In families one can deal with individuals; in societies one must deal with groups when statistical alternatives emerge from the fog that make policy management possible. Here numbers are the arbiter of policy and the individual has become not just faceless but virtually invisible.

RELATED ANECDOTES

FURTHER READING

Durkheim, Émile. *Suicide: A Study in Sociology.* Glencoe: Free, 1951.

Henslin, James M. *Essentials of Sociology.* Needham Heights: Allyn and Bacon, 1996.

Thompson, Kenneth. *Émile Durkheim.* 2nd ed. London: Routledge, 2002.

73

THE MONKEY'S PAW

IN A CLASSIC 1902 novella of this title, the English writer W. W. Jacobs (1863–1943) projected a macabre story that, in briefest outline, runs as follows: A man acquires a monkey's paw, a magic talisman that gives its possessor the chance to realize three wishes. He proceeds to exploit this opportunity. But his first two wishes, though realized, are achieved in so horrendous a way and at such a terrible price that his third and final wish was simply for the whole thing to go away.

The first lesson here relates to the complexity of human desire. We not only want what we wish for, but we also want our wishes to be realized on our own terms.

And the second lesson is that we often fail to recognize when we are well off. For it can all too readily happen that improving this or that aspect of our condition is something that can be realized only at the price of accepting other changes that exact a more than proportionate price.

Then too there is the further lesson that it lies in the nature of things that the natural order cannot be perfect. For as Plato already insisted, the imperfectability of the natural universe is an inevitable aspect of its materiality, its physical embodiment (*somatoeides*).[1] And here it is followed in this view by a substantial Neo-Platonic tradition that endures to our own day.[2]

"But could not the amount of human suffering that there is in the world be reduced?" For sure it could. But then the question is: At what cost? At the price of there being no world at all? At the price of there being no humans in the world? At the price of having all humans be ignorant, obtuse, and unintelligent? At the price of having only humans without empathy, sympathy, and care for one another? The proper response to all of these questions is simply: Who knows? No one can say with any assurance that the cost of such an "improvement" would be acceptable. Granted, the world's *particular* negativities may in theory be remediable. But to arrange for this may well require accepting an even larger array of negativities overall (the Monkey's Paw effect). The cost in collateral damage of avoiding those manifest evils of this world would then be the realization of an even larger volume of misfortune. Such a Neo-Platonic position is effectively what Leibniz propounded long ago: it does not claim that the world is *perfect*, but just that it is *optimal*—"the best possible," with the emphasis not on *best* but on *possible*.

RELATED ANECDOTES

FURTHER READING

Jacobs, W. W. *The Monkey's Paw and Other Tales.* Chicago: Academy, 1997.
Rescher, Nicholas. *Axiogenesis: An Essay in Metaphysical Optimalism.* Lanham: Lexington, 2010.

---

1.   Plato, *Politics,* 273B. Even—indeed especially—in the sunlight will material objects cast a shadow. See Plotinus, *Enneads,* III, 2.5.
2.   See Plato, *Timaeus* 28C, 35A, 50D.

74

WELLS'S NEOMEN

CHARLES DARWIN'S THEORY OF evolution revolutionized thought about man's place in nature. As a scientific theory geared to the observational facts, it had, of course, to be based on the history of past developments. But it also invited speculation about the prospects and possibilities of the future. For here, the prospect of genetic manipulation at the personal and social level raises a host of philosophically laden sociopolitical and ethical issues regarding justice, ethical obligation, and the nature of the good life for humankind.

The thinker who took up this invitation most notably was the English writer and polymath H. G. Wells (1866–1946) in his classic story *The Time Machine*. At its core lay the following speculation: The course of future biological and social evolution witnesses an eventual split of the human race into two branches: the Eloi, an intellectual caste of sophisticated creatures living a life of ease in pleasant surroundings, and the Morlocks, a brutish but hardworking caste of cave dwellers—"something inhuman and malign." Evolution had been at work, and the "too perfect security of the overworld had led these to a slow movement of degeneration at last—to a general dwindling of size, strength, and intelligence."[1] However, while facilitating the easy life of the Eloi, these Morlocks were not subservient to them in the sociopolitical sense. Rather this "lesser" caste served their evolutionary cousins as food!

Many philosophically instructive lessons are inherent in Wells's challenging tale. One is that the future—and especially the distant future—is contingent, unpredictable, imponderable, and perhaps even unimaginable within the thought categories of the present. Another idea is that not only will the life conditions of the future be radically different from our own but also that even the value scheme of our eventual positivity may be radically different. And here it will be highly problematic to judge the value system of one era by the standards of another.

Exercising our imagination about the future is generally interesting and often tempting. But the fact remains that if we do not heed the limits of plausibility and venture too far out into the sea of conjecture, then we are rudderless in an uneasy sea. Speculative futurology is even riskier than counterfactual history.

RELATED ANECDOTES

FURTHER READING

Charlesworth, C. B., and D. Charlesworth. *Evolution*. Oxford: Oxford University Press 2003.

Larson, E. J. *Evolution: The Remarkable History of Scientific Theory*. New York: Modern Library, 2004.

Shaw, G. B. *Man and Superman*. Many editions.

Wells, H. G. *The Time Machine*. New York: Henry Holt, 1895.

---

1. H. G. Wells, *The Time Machine* (New York: Henry Holt, 1895), 118.

75

BOREL'S MONKEYS

IN HIS 1914 BOOK *On Chance* (*Le hasard*), the French mathematician Émile Borel (1871–1956) projected the image of an array of typing monkeys, proceeding along the following lines: Suppose there be a vast office with a thousand rows each with a thousand work desks, all of them equipped with a typewriter. And suppose that a million monkeys are seated at these typewriters, each of them pecking away randomly for ten hours each day for years on end. It would still remain unlikely that their efforts would yield a meaningful book. And it would be unlikely to the verge of impossibility that they would replicate the contents of a large library.

Soon, however, other theorists came along to insist that if they kept at it sufficiently long, then those monkeys would indeed eventually replicate the works of Shakespeare.

Any attempt to transmute the typing monkey scenario into an actual experiment in the real world will encounter not only practical but also theoretical obstacles. For the argumentation of the infinite monkey theorem of probability mathematics is predicated on the supposition of actual randomness in proceeding. But this is a tall order. For example, suppose those monkeys have a dislike for the letter Z and systematically avoid it. Then no matter how long or how much they type, a text containing even a single Z will never result.

Randomness is a very special condition that is not automatically ensured in nature's ventures into disorder. Granted, where pure randomness exists and endures, it is, in the end, bound to produce results of immense improbability. But with any particular process—be it natural or conceptual—the question "Is it actually altogether random?" is always open.

There is no question that chance plays a prominent and perhaps even predominant role in human life from start to finish. And it is certainly not something we can control. On the other hand, we can court its favor ("You can't win the lottery if you don't buy a ticket") and guard against its malice (for example, by insuring ourselves against various hazards). But one thing is certain about the favor of chance and luck: we should never count on it.

RELATED ANECDOTES

FURTHER READING

Borel, Émile. *Elements of the Theory of Probability.* Englewood Cliffs: Prentice-Hall, 1965.

Borges, Jorge Luis. "The Total Library." In *J. L. Borges: Selected Non-Fictions.* Translated by Eliot Wernberger. London: Penguin, 1999.

Rescher, Nicholas. "Leibniz on Coordinating Epistemology and Ontology." In *Studies in Quantitative Philosophizing,* 131–60. Frankfurt: ONTOS, 2010.

Rescher, Nicholas. *Luck.* New York: Farrar, Straus and Giroux, 1995.

76

RUSSELL'S KING OF FRANCE

THE ENGLISH PHILOSOPHER AND logician Bertrand Russell (1872–1970) was entranced by the puzzle of meaningful discourse about things that do not exist—and perhaps even cannot possibly exist. This problem had already figured in Plato's dialogues,[1] and had recently been reactivated by the Austrian philosopher Alexius Meinong (1853–1920). After all, it would seem that meaningful discourse must be *about something*—and how can this be if the thing purportedly at issue just isn't there? Russell accordingly protested:

> [Meinong's] theory regards any grammatically correct denoting phrase as standing for an *object*. Thus "the present King of France," "the round square," etc., are supposed to be genuine objects. It is admitted that such objects do not subsist, but nevertheless they are supposed to be objects. This is in itself a difficult view; but the chief objection is that such objects, admittedly, are apt to infringe the law of contradiction. It is contended, for example, that the existent present King of France exists, and also does not exist; that the round square is round, and also not round; etc. But

1. See especially the dialogues *Parmenides*, *Theaetetus*, and *Sophist* (especially *Sophist* 236E).

this is intolerable; and if any theory can be found to avoid this result, it is surely to be preferred.[2]

To implement this perspective, Russell propounded his Theory of Descriptions. Its core was the *contextual definition* that a certain property *P* can be truly ascribed to an individual *N* described as "the *x* having the property *F*" whenever it can be shown that:

(1) *some* individual has *F*,
(2) *at most* one individual has *F*,
(3) and that every individual having *F* also has *P*

On this basis the attribution of properties to nonexistents vanishes as a viable prospect because that first presupposition is always false.

Unfortunately this tactic is not very helpful for thinking about these issues. For even as Russell is dismayed by the fact that, in the standard account, all propriety attributes are (trivially) true, so we now have it on his own account that they are all (trivially) false, because that fact requisite uniformly fails to hold. Thus "the present king of France is a king" is just as false as the claim that he is a commoner. And the truism "the husband of Queen Elizabeth I was married to her" is now a falsehood rather than a truism. Such consequences of this account look to be as anomalous as those Russell is purporting to remove. In its attempt to provide a synoptic one-size-fits-all construal of discourse about nonexistents, Russell embarked on one generalization too far.

In an influential 1948 paper titled "On What There Is" the Harvard philosopher W. V. Quine (1908–2000) sought to throw cold water on the whole issue of nonexistents:

> Take, for instance, the possible fat man in that doorway and, again, the possible bald man in the doorway. Are they the same possible man, or two possible men? How do we decide? How many possible men are in that doorway? Are there more possible thin ones than fat ones? How many of them are alike? Or would their being alike make them one? Are no *two* possible things alike? Or, finally, is the concept of identity simply inapplicable to unactualized possibles? But what sense can be found in talking of entities which cannot meaningfully be said to be identical with themselves and distinct from one another? These elements

---

2. Bertrand Russell, "On Denoting," *Mind* 14 (1965): 483.

are well-nigh incorrigible. By a Fregean therapy of individual concepts, some effort might be made at rehabilitation; but I feel we'd do better simply to clear this slum and be done with it.[3]

In principle, the answer to Quine's question would appear to be straightforward:

- In actuality there are none.
- In possibility there are many, but only one at a time, given the (hypothetical) size of fat men and the (hypothetical) width of the doorway.
- Still, that putative fat man can be any one of an endlessly describable infinitude of possible alternatives. Any one of zillions could be there—though only one at a time.

All of this is pretty much a matter of common sense with little logical sophistication required.

Nevertheless, a significant lesson emerges here. Unrealism breeds perplexity. The further our fact-contravening hypotheses are distinct from the accepted actual reality of things, the more problematic it will be to make reasonable judgments about the matter. We are creatures of cognitive as well as of biological evolution. Our thought and its linguistic instrumentalities have developed to help us deal with the reality of things as best we can determine it. The further we leave behind us the secure ground of what we accept as true, the wider we open the door to puzzling complications.

RELATED ANECDOTES

FURTHER READING

Grayling, A. C. *Bertrand Russell.* Oxford: Oxford University Press, 1996.

Quine, W. V. *From a Logical Point of View.* Cambridge: Harvard University Press, 1953.

Quine, W. V. "On What There Is." *Review of Metaphysics* 2 (1948): 21–38.

Rescher, Nicholas. "The Concept of Nonexistent Possible." *Essays on Philosophical Analysis.* Pittsburgh: University of Pittsburgh Press, 1969.

Russell, Bertrand. "On Denoting." *Mind* 14 (1965): 479–93.

---

3.   W. V. Quine, "On What There Is," *Review of Metaphysics* 2 (1948): 23–24.

77

RUSSELL'S CHICKEN

INDUCTIVE REASONING EXHIBITS OUR inherent tendency to expect the patterns of past occurrence to continue in the future. And here Bertrand Russell urged a skeptical perspective: "Expectations of uniformity are liable to be misleading. The man who has fed the chicken every day throughout its life at last wrings its neck, showing that more refined views as to the uniformity of nature would have been useful to the chicken."[1]

We may put aside for the present the question of how the chicken would have profited from this knowledge, as well as the old joke about the man who fell from the top of the skyscraper and felt increasingly secure as he passed story after story without incident. The fact remains, however, that there are two sorts of manifolds, those that, like numbers or hours, are inexhaustible and those that, like stories in a building or weeks in an agrarian cycle, are limited in number and thereby exhaustible. No doubt a second-order induction is needed to determine in particular cases what sort of manifold is at issue so that a course of sensible inductive reasoning can be

---

1.   Bertrand Russell, *The Problems of Philosophy* (Oxford: Oxford University Press, 1912), 98.

conducted. Like any other general procedure in rational inference, induction is a method that must be practiced with care. But the prospect of its misuse does not negate the usefulness of a procedure.

RELATED ANECDOTES

FURTHER READING

Kyburg, Henry E., Jr. *Probability and Inductive Logic*. New York: Macmillan, 1970.

Rescher, Nicholas. *Induction*. Oxford: Blackwell, 1980.

Russell, Bertrand. *The Problems of Philosophy*. Oxford: Oxford University Press, 1912.

78

ANGELL'S ILLUSION

ONE OF THE MOST widely admired and discussed works of
the early twentieth century was a booklet by the English economic
theorist and political philosopher (and Nobel Prize laureate) Norman Angell (1872–1967). Published in 1910 and titled *The Great
Illusion,* the book had a simple and telling thesis, which ran roughly
as follows: The principal modern industrial powers have economies
whose effective functioning is extensively interconnected and inter-
dependent, and the means of modern warfare are so destructive that
war among these nations makes no possible sense. No power will
gain from it—all will lose out: no one will emerge in a better condition than would otherwise have been the case. A major modern war
would have no victors but only victims. The reality of it is that war
does not pay.

In the words of its second edition synopsis, Angell's books
sought to show that military conquest in war is pointless:

> The author challenges this whole doctrine. . . . It belongs to a stage
> of development out of which we have passed that the commerce
> and industry of a people no longer depend upon the expansion
> of its political frontiers; that a nation's political and economic

frontiers do not now necessarily coincide; that military power is socially and economically futile, and can have no relation to the prosperity of the people exercising it; that it is impossible for one nation to seize by force the wealth or trade of another—to enrich itself by subjugating, to impose its will by force on another; that, in short, war, even when victorious, can no longer achieve those aims for which peoples strive.[1]

Since Immanuel Kant's day, arguments against war have generally proceeded on humanitarian and ethical grounds. By contrast, Angell's reasoning was shortly prudential and economic in its tenor. Simply put, his thesis was that *war does not pay*—especially given modern methods of virtually industrial destructiveness. Neither does war generally realize the objective for whose sake nations enter upon it, nor do the resulting benefits to the creativeness involved compensate for the loss of life and treasure that results. Initially published on the eve of World War I, Angell's prescient point was soon vividly illustrated by the physical, social, and human carnage that played out after August 1914.

One thing that Angell did not and could not have reckoned with, however, is the transformation of war's rationale that lay around the corner. For while most modern wars had, in the main, been fought for gain in terms of territory and power, those of the present day hark back to the earlier era of conflicts of religion. And these intangible motivations were a great deal less susceptible to the controls of reason through the guidance of prudence and good sense.

RELATED ANECDOTES

FURTHER READING

Angell, Norman. *The Great Illusion*. 2nd ed. London: W. Heinemann, 1935.
Singer J. D., and Melvin Small. *The Wages of War, 1816–1965: A Statistical Handbook*. New York: Wiley and Sons, 1972.

---

1. Norman Angell, *The Great Illusion,* 2nd ed. (London: W. Heinemann, 1935), synopsis.

79

RICHARDSON'S COASTLINE

THE ENGLISH MATHEMATICIAN AND scientist Lewis Fry Richardson (1881–1953) posed the seemingly innocuous question "How long is the coast of Britain?," and he arrived at a seemingly paradoxical answer: No finite quantity can possibly afford an adequate measure here. The distance must be adjudged infinite. For between any two points, there will be zigs, zags, squiggles, and wiggles that constantly increase the apparent distance of those points from one another.

In fact even the preliminary question "Just where is the coast of Britain?" would seem to be unanswerable. Not only are there those uncertainly shifting tides, but every splash and wavelet alters the boundary between water and land in such a way that the border is never fixed more than instantaneously: like mercury it slips away the instant you put your finger on it.

And many other seeming "quantities" are in the same boat; for example, just what is a person's *exact* age (to the nearest nanosecond) or their *exact* height (to the nearest nanometer)? The "quantities" at issue in such matters perhaps only qualify as *quasi*-quantities because they are ultimately indefinite and imprecise; they simply disallow any prospect of exact specification.

When confronting such indeterminate quantities we have two choices. One is to say that the quantity at issue just does not exist as such—that, for example, there is no such thing as the exact length of the British coastline or the exact weight of a person—"at a particular time" in either case. (Or, for that matter, that there is no such thing as "the exact time right now.") This approach dismisses the quantity at issue as being no more than a convenient fiction.

The other approach is to accept the quantity as ontologically real but epistemically inaccessible—as actual but unknowable. This view of the matter assimilates these indefinite quantities to predicative vagrancy. One can take the line that just as there indeed are facts that are unknown to me—though of course I cannot specifically instantiate them as such—so there indeed is an exact weight that I now have but that simply cannot be specified.

Either way, there remains the philosophically significant point that there is a potential disconnect between the quantities we standardly involve in everyday communication and those that are theoretically appropriate. In consequence we must always be ever mindful of the important distinction between what is cogent in theory and what is adequate to our needs in practice.

RELATED ANECDOTES

FURTHER READING

Kosto, Bart. *Fuzzy Thinking: The New Science of Fuzzy Logic*. New York: Hyperion, 1993.

Rescher, Nicholas. *Epistemic Logic*. Pittsburgh: University of Pittsburgh Press, 2005.

Van Pelt, Miles. *Fuzzy Logic Applied to Daily Life*. Seattle: No No No No Press, 2008.

80

DUCHAMP'S URINAL

IN 1917 THE FRENCH art theorist Marcel Duchamp (1887–1968) had a peculiar inspiration: Duchamp purchased a urinal made by the T. L. Mutt iron works, signed it R. Mutt, and submitted it to an exhibition organized by the Society of Independent Artists in New York. Titled *Fountain*, it was to be laid flat on its side rather than mounted in its standard upright position. And its inclusion in the exhibit created an uproar.

Intended as a work of provocation, Duchamp's urinal has rightly been termed "the practical joke that launched an artistic revolution." There was, however, method in Duchamp's madness. He sought to downgrade and dismiss much artistic creation as "retinal art" that merely sought to please the eye. In its stead, he advocated for "cerebral art" designed to elicit responses in the mind. As he saw it, the proper function of art is not to evoke feeling but to provoke thought. And this envisioned a turning from classicism to modernity.

Of course the art-consuming public reacted with fury and outrage (something not altogether unwelcome to the attention-seeking exhibitors—let alone to those enterprising art aficionados for whom *épater le bourgeois* had lately become the pinnacle of sophistication). But theorists responded with delight because the uproar added much grist to the mill of the chattering theory-driven classes in the form of questions about the nature, function, and limits of art; however, the episode had another significant aspect.

Traditionally, there were three prime stakeholders in the domain of art:

the creative artists
the consuming audience
the art patrons and collectors

But in the course of the twentieth century, various other stakeholders became prominent upon the scene:

art critics and "art appreciation" theorists
art history teachers
art followers and "groupies"
art dealers, collectors, and investors
art promoters and career developers

The roles of the traditional audience of art consumers has come to play an ever decreasing role in the wider setting of the "art world."

The increasing complexity of life in modern advanced societies that has transformed the traditional shape of economic and social life has imposed upon the realm of cultural affairs as well. And in its wake the role that art nowadays plays in the lives of individuals has become transformed with the senses increasingly yielding to the intellect as a focus of appeal.

RELATED ANECDOTES

1. The Tower of Babel   7
74. Wells's Neomen   210
101. Derrida's Demolition   282

FURTHER READING

Danton, Arthur C. *After the End of Art.* Princeton: Princeton University Press, 1997.
Tomkins, Calvin. *Duchamp: A Biography.* New York: Henry Holt, 1996.

81

WITTGENSTEIN'S POKER

FROM THE SKEPTICS OF classical antiquity to the scientistic positivists of the nineteenth century and the logical positivists of the twentieth, there has been an ongoing chain of thinkers drawn to the idea that all (other) philosophizing is a futile and misconceived endeavor, seeing that a cognitive enterprise that does not issue in consensus thereby manifests its illegitimacy. In this regard, a brief argument between two major twentieth-century thinkers has had substantial repercussions in the philosophical arena. On the evening of Friday, October 25, 1946, the Cambridge Moral Science Club, a philosophy discussion group, met to hear a general lecture by Karl Popper (1902–1994) on the topic "Are There Philosophical Problems?" Among those present were Bertrand Russell (1872–1970) and Ludwig Wittgenstein (1889–1951), two of the day's most celebrated philosophers.[1]

Popper's topic was a torpedo aimed straight at Wittgenstein, who was widely viewed as a philosophical nihilist who regarded the

---

1. The whole episode is elaborately discussed in David Edmonds and John Eidinow, *Wittgenstein's Poker* (London: Faber and Faber, 2001).

established range of philosophical problems as rooted in misunderstandings of fact and language and, insofar as meaningful, addressing matters that properly belong to the sciences.

The secretary of the society recorded the gist of the discussion:

> POPPER: Wittgenstein and his school never venture beyond preliminaries, for which they claimed the title philosophy, to address the more important problems of philosophy. . . . And he gave some examples of difficulties whose resolution required delving beneath the surface of language.
> WITTGENSTEIN: These are no more than problems in pure mathematics or sociology.
> AUDIENCE: Unconvinced by Popper's examples. Atmosphere charged. Unusual degree of controversy. Some very vocal.[2]

After Popper had opened, Wittgenstein rose to respond. What happened has been described as follows:

> Wittgenstein's hand had gone to the hearth and tightened around the poker, its tip surrounded by ash and tiny cinders, as Braithwaite had left it earlier. The dons watched anxiously as Wittgenstein picked it up and began convulsively jabbing with it to punctuate his statements. Braithwaite had seen him do it before. This time Wittgenstein seemed especially agitated, even physically uncomfortable—unaccustomed to a guest's counterpunching, perhaps. By this stage of a meeting he was usually in the full flood that people complained about behind his back. Things were beginning to look somewhat out of control. Someone—was it Russell?—said: "Wittgenstein, put the poker down." . . . The door slammed behind Wittgenstein.[3]

The ramifications of this extraordinary episode convey a few instructive lessons. The first is that few philosophical problems are as extensively and boldly contested as is the nature of philosophy itself: its mission, its methods, and its prospects. So here we have what is—curiously enough—itself one of the key questions of philosophy, namely, "What is it that constitutes an appropriate philosophical question or problem?"

---

2.   Edmonds and Eidinow, *Wittgenstein's Poker*, 269.

3.   Edmonds and Eidinow, *Wittgenstein's Poker*, 269.

The historical answer to this question would look to what has always been regarded among the main avenues of human endeavor, namely, matters of belief, action, evaluation, and practice. And proceeding in this direction one could ask the following kinds of questions: Are all beliefs created equal? Or are those valid considerations to indicate that some are better warranted than others? And if so, what are the considerations at issue here? And of course analogous questions can be posed within each of those other three aforementioned departments.

There are, to be sure, the not uncommon individuals of scientistic inclination who (with Wittgenstein) hold that if a question is meaningful at all (or, as they would prefer to say, *empirically* meaningful), then one must turn to the sciences for an answer. But the all-too-obvious problem here is that there simply is no science that addresses questions of the aforementioned sort.

RELATED ANECDOTES

FURTHER READING

Edmonds, David, and John Eidinow. *Wittgenstein's Poker.* London: Faber and Faber, 2001.

Kenny, Anthony. *Wittgenstein.* Cambridge: Harvard University Press, 1973.

Passmore, John. *A Hundred Years of Philosophy.* New York: Basic, 1966.

82

COLLINGWOOD'S PRESUPPOSITIONS

ARISTOTLE MAINTAINED THAT KNOWLEDGE begins in wonder, and in this spirit it is often said that all knowledge issues from questioning. The inverse thesis that questions always issue from beliefs—that every question has some prepositional presupposition—is also in prospect.

Following in Aristotle's footsteps, the British historian and philosopher R. G. Collingwood (1889–1943) maintained that "Every statement that anybody ever makes is made in answer to a question." But he also went on to maintain that "Every question involves a presupposition," seeing that, after all, it cannot but presuppose—among other things—that it indeed has a meaningful and true answer.[1] And so, even as the classic query "Have you stopped beating your wife?" is predicated on a rather presumptuous precondition, so Collingwood maintained that:

> Every question involves a presupposition. It may be doubted whether any question that was ever asked involved one presupposition and no more. Ordinarily a question involves large

---

1. R. G. Collingwood, *An Essay on Metaphysics* (Oxford: Clarendon, 1940), 23, 25, 28.

numbers of them. But distinction should be made between what a question involves directly and what it involves indirectly. Directly or immediately any given question involves one presupposition and only one, namely, that from which it directly and immediately "arises." This immediate presupposition, however, has in turn other presuppositions, which are thus indirectly presupposed by the original question. Unless this immediate presupposition were made, the question to which it is logically immediately prior could not be logically asked.[2]

Collingwood then went on to project the idea of *absolute presuppositions*, which are never themselves the answers to questions and the facts of inquiry but represent commitments assumed in order to open up a line of questioning and investigation. And Collingwood regarded such absolutes as central issues in philosophy.

But now, of course, we arrive at a chicken-and-egg–style puzzle. For it would seem that to legitimate a question one must first establish certain facts (namely, those at issue in its presuppositions), and to establish those facts one must first raise various questions about the matters at issue. To all appearances we seem to be caught up in a vicious cycle. But here appearances can be deceitful, for we can avert perplexity by drawing a distinction.

The fact is that there are two versions of presupposition: the *temporal* is something that must be done first, and the *coordinative* merely requires conjunction. When I say that baking a cake presupposes the acquisition of flour, I claim that this is something that must be done first, in advance of baking. But when I say that being a parent presupposes the existence of children, I am not claiming that those children must (or even can) preexist their parents.

When *A*'s being so presupposes *B*'s being so (for example, being a parent presupposes having a child), this does not mean the latter does not have temporal precedence over the former. Their arrangement in time may be temporally coordinate (as with motherhood and childbearing) or even atemporal (as being a circle presupposes having a center).

Collingwood then proceeded to elaborate a vision of the nature of philosophy, focusing on metaphysics as its key component: "metaphysics is the attempt to find out what absolute presupposi-

---

2. Collingwood, *An Essay on Metaphysics*, 25.

tions have been made by this or that person or group of persons, on this or that occasion or group of occasions, in the course of this or that piece of thinking. . . . All metaphysical questions are historical questions. Every metaphysical question is simply the question which absolute presuppositions were made on a certain occasion, and is capable of being resolved into a number of such questions."[3]

The rather bizarre nature of this position leaps at once to the eye. For why should it be that our attention should always dwell on either persons or times? Why limit philosophers to being historians? Why cannot a philosopher ask, What absolute presuppositions figure in our own proceedings and with what justification is it that we proceed in this way? What, for us, here and now, are the *appropriate* presuppositions, and how is it that we should fix upon these as so qualified?

It is, all too obviously, this sort of issue that requires the attention of the philosopher not just as a historian, who reports what people have thought, but rather as a thinker in his own right. This is an issue that Collingwood does not confront as such—and perhaps cannot confront within the limits of his own doctrinal commitments.

Immanuel Kant said at the outset of his *Prolegomena to Any Future Metaphysic* that "there are those scholars for whom the history of philosophy (ancient and modern included) is itself what constitutes philosophy."[4] Collingwood was perhaps one of them.

RELATED ANECDOTES

FURTHER READING

Collingwood, R. G. *An Autobiography*. Oxford: Clarendon, 1939.
Collingwood, R. G. *An Essay on Metaphysics*. Oxford: Clarendon, 1940.
Johnson, Peter. *R. G. Collingwood: An Introduction*. Bristol: Thoemmes, 1998.

---

3. Collingwood, *An Essay on Metaphysics*, 217–49.
4. Immanuel Kant, *Prolegomena to Any Future Metaphysic*, trans. L. W. Beck (Indianapolis: Bobbs-Merrill, 1950), preface.

83

COLLINGWOOD'S
HISTORY TRAP

IT SEEMS THAT PHILOSOPHERS, like politicians, fall into warring tribes. In antiquity we have Aristotelians and Platonists, Stoics and Epicureans; in the Middle Ages, Thomists and Augustinians and Scotists; in modern times, Rationalists and Empiricists, and so on. Or so it seems. However, some theorists have argued that these appearances are misleading. What seem to be conflicting philosophical doctrines are in fact—so they contend—totally separate positions that neither agree nor disagree but are actually incomparable or incommensurable. Such discordant positions—so these incommensurability theorists maintain—simply cannot be brought into contact with one another; they cannot be compared in point of agreement or contradiction because no common measure of comparison can be established between them.

On such a view, different philosophers do not actually form schools that hold divergent views on essentially the same issues— they share no issues and live in disjoint cognitive domains that share no common territory. Rival doctrinal positions are totally disconnected; different theories are incommensurable—they cannot be expressed in common units of thought. Adherents of different theories literally live in different thought worlds, among which contact—be it by way of disagreement or agreement—is simply impossible.

In the English-language orbit, the prime spokesman for such a view was R. G. Collingwood:

> If there were a permanent problem P, we could ask What did Kant, or Leibniz, or Berkeley, think about P? And if that question could be answered, we could then go on to ask was Kant, or Leibniz, or Berkeley right in what he thought about P? But what is thought to be a permanent problem P is really a number of transitory problems, $P_1, P_2, P_3, \ldots$ whose individual peculiarities are blurred by the historical myopia of the person who lumps them together under the name P.[1]

Various intellectual historians have shared this point of view, maintaining that every thinker stands alone—that every teaching is ultimately distinctive, every thesis so imprinted with the characteristic thought style of its proponent that no two thinkers ever discuss the same proposition. Disagreement—indeed even comprehension—across doctrinal divides becomes impossible: the thought of every thinker stands apart in splendid isolation. Discordant philosophers can never be said to contribute to the same ongoing issues: "There are simply no perennial problems in philosophy: there are only individual answers to individual questions, with as many different answers as there are questions, and as many different questions as there are questioners."[2] Philosophers of different persuasions are separated from each other by an unbridgeable gulf of mutual incomprehension. So argue the theorists of doctrinal incommensurability.

There is, however, good reason to think that this view exaggerates mutual incomprehension to the point of absurdity. Of course, incomprehension *can* and sometimes *does* occur across reaches of time or space when major conceptual dissimilarities are involved. But this is certainly not the case generally or necessarily. To insist that deliberations about the nature and function of the law in St. Thomas Aquinas are incommensurable with those in Kant is

1. R. G. Collingwood, *An Autobiography* (Oxford: Clarendon, 1939), 69.
2. John Herman Randall, *The Career of Philosophy* (New York: Columbia University Press, 1962–1965), 50.

like saying that the Alps and the Rockies cannot both be mountain ranges because they are so different. After all, the very question before us—"Can philosophers disagree and how should this be so?"— is itself one with which philosophers have grappled time and again.

To deny the possibility of philosophical disagreement is to abandon the enterprise as a meaningful cognitive project from the very outset. For where there is no prospect of disagreement, there is no prospect of agreement either. Without the prospect of shared problems and theses considered in common by diverse thinkers, all hope of interpretation and comprehension is lost. If conceptual contact across the divide of conflicting beliefs were impossible, then, given the diversity of their views, all philosophers would be condemned to mutual incomprehension. Every thinker—indeed each one of us—would be locked within the impenetrable walls of our own thought world. If one philosophical mind cannot connect with another, then *we* ourselves cannot connect with anyone either. In the absence of relatability to other times and places, the historian would be faced with issues that they are incapable of dealing with. If Kant cannot address Hume's problems, neither can Collingwood. We ourselves would be condemned to philosophical solipsism— unable to make a rational assessment of the ideas of any other thinker due to an inability to make conceptual contact. And if philosophers cannot speak to one another, then they cannot speak to us either.

RELATED ANECDOTES

FURTHER READING

Collingwood, R. G. *An Autobiography*. Oxford: Clarendon, 1939.

Collingwood, R. G. *Speculum Mentis*. Oxford: Clarendon, 1924.

Inglis, Fred. *History Man: The Life of R. G. Collingwood*. Princeton: Princeton University Press, 2009.

Johnson, Peter. *Collingwood's* The Idea of History: *A Reader's Guide*. London: Bloomsbury, 2013.

Randall, John Herman. *The Career of Philosophy*. New York: Columbia University Press, 1962–1965.

84

TEILHARD'S OMEGA

THE FRENCH SCHOLAR AND scientist Teilhard de Chardin (1898–1955) had an unusual mix of interests and talents, being at once a paleontologist, a philosopher, and a theologian.

A priest and member of the Society of Jesus, Teilhard's theological ideas were disapproved of and condemned in official Catholic circles during his lifetime, but the grandeur of his vision and the sincerity of his Christology posthumously gained him respect and admiration at the highest levels.

Teilhard's grand conception is that of the Omega Point, a teleologically concerned end state of cosmic evolution in which there is an ultimate merging of man, nature, and divine spirit: a fusing where biological evolution, cognitive motivation, and spiritual function coalesce into a harmonious synthesis in the diamatizing of cosmic development.

Teilhard thus envisioned a grand unfolding of the world historical process where biological development, cosmic evolution, and theological eschatology come together in a grand synthesis of teleological ultimacy.

Teilhard formulated the matter as follows:

We have seen and admitted that evolution is an ascent towards consciousness. That is no longer contested even by the most materialistic, or at all events by the most agnostic of humanitarians. *Therefore it should culminate forwards in some sort of supreme consciousness.* . . .

All our difficulties and repulsions as regards the opposition between the All and the Person would be dissipated if only we understood that, by structure, the noosphere (and more generally the world) represent a whole that is not only closed but also *centred.* Because it contains and engenders consciousness, space-time is necessarily *of a convergent nature.* Accordingly its enormous layers, followed in the right direction, must somewhere ahead become involuted to a point which we might call *Omega,* which fuses and consumes them integrally in itself. . . .

Thus it would be mistaken to represent Omega to ourselves simply as a centre born of the fusion of elements which it collects, or annihilating them in itself. By its structure Omega, in its ultimate principle, can only be *a distinct Centre radiating at the core of a system of centres;* a grouping in which personalisation of the All and personalisations of the elements reach their maximum, simultaneously and without merging, under the influence of a supremely autonomous focus of union.[1]

Along these lines Teilhard envisioned a fusion of Platonism's intelligent design with evolutionary biology and monotheistic theology. His many-faceted positions vividly show that even at this late hour it is still possible—albeit difficult—for serious scholars and scientists to swim against the stream of predominant opinion without a total loss of credibility.

RELATED ANECDOTES

---

1. Teilhard de Chardin, *The Phenomenon of Man* (New York: Harper, 1976), 258–63.

FURTHER READING

Chardin, Teilhard de. *The Divine Milieu*. New York: Harper, 2001.
Chardin, Teilhard de. *The Phenomenon of Man*. New York: Harper, 1976.
Grumett, David. *Teilhard de Chardin*. Dudley: Peeters, 2005.
Spaight, Robert. *The Life of Teilhard de Chardin*. New York: Harper and Row, 1967.

PART 5

THE CURRENT ERA, 1900 TO THE PRESENT

85

SCI-FI PSYCHOLOGY

THE LARGE AND DIVERSIFIED literature of science fiction raises a host of curious brain manipulation issues along the lines of the following scenario: A perverse operative—mad scientist or wicked governmental agency—devises a brain wave transfer apparatus that interchanges the memories, tastes, likings, longings, or even total knowledge of one individual with that of another.

Given this situation, the issues that now arise are which is which and who is who? The very concept of personal identity is thus brought into question. For example, does sameness of person depend on physical or on psychic continuity?

With this sort of issue in view, the contemporary literature of the philosophy of mind has witnessed an android invasion. Its landscape is full of robots whose communicative behavior is remarkably anthropoidal (are they "conscious" or not?) and of personality exchanges between people (which one is "the same person"?). In examining such issues, theorists purport to be clarifying the conceptions at issue. But all such proceedings are actually of very dubious significance. For the assumptions at issue force apart what normally goes together—and do so in circumstances where the concepts we use are predicated upon a certain background of "normality."

In the end, no supposedly clarificatory hypothesis should arbitrarily cut asunder what the basic facts of this world have joined together—at any rate not when trying to elucidate the concepts whose very being are predicated on those facts. For in the normal course of things, those coordinated concepts are what function, (generally) resolved only by the favorable cooperation of empirical circumstance where the tension that might in theory only be because the facts (as we see them) are duly cooperative. But once we forgo reliance on these facts in the interests of theoretical neatness, the tension becomes destructive. For those attempted "clarifications" by the use of extreme cases and fanciful science-fiction examples engender pressures that burst the bonds that hold our concepts together. When we put reality aside and embark on far-fetched hypotheses, unmanageable difficulties crowd in upon us.

The tragic destiny of philosophy is to be constrained to pursue the interests of abstract rationality by means of concepts designed to accommodate the facts of experience; to have to probe the merely possible with the thought instruments that have evolved to handle the concretely actual; to be constrained to address the necessary in the language of the contingent. In philosophy we have to be prepared for approximation and analogies that limit our generalizations to the normal and ordinary course of things. Hypotheses that cast our understanding of the world's ways to the winds thereby annihilate the very concepts in whose terms our deliberations must be conducted.

RELATED ANECDOTES

FURTHER READING

Chisholm, Roderick M. *Person and Object*. Chicago: Open Court, 1976.

Miller, Fred D., Jr., and Nicholas D. Smith. *Thought Probes*. Englewood Cliffs: Prentice-Hall, 1980.

Rescher, Nicholas. *Philosophical Standardism*. Pittsburgh: University of Pittsburgh Press, 1994.

Shoemaker, Sydney, and Richard Swinburne. *Personal Identity*. Oxford: Blackwell, 1984.

86

AYER'S NONSENSE

THE LOGICAL POSITIVISTS OF the 1930s were unabashedly scientific ideologists for whom the observational verification of our factual claims was not just a determinant of their truth but an indispensable prerequisite standard of meaningfulness. In the Anglophone realm, A. J. Ayer (1910–1989) was their prime spokesperson and he framed the matter in stark terms as follows: "If a putative proposition fails to satisfy this principle [of observational verifiability] and is not a [mere] tautology, then I hold that it is metaphysical, and then being metaphysical it is neither true nor false, but literally senseless."[1] Observational verifiability was held to be the *hallmark* of meaningfulness for all substantive discourse, thereby annihilating as meaningless verbiage the greater part of traditional philosophizing, derisively branded as "metaphysical."

The problem that defeated this positivist demarche on meaning was that of boundary demarcation. For the course of developments showed that no workable conception of verifiability could effect an acceptable division between philosophical speculation on the one

---

1.   A. J. Ayer, *Language, Truth and Logic* (New York: Dover, 1952), introduction.

side and scientific theorizing on the other. Every proposal for implementing the idea of observational testability resulted in throwing out some scientific babies along with the metaphysical bathwater.

Just where are the limits of verifiability to be positioned? In *practical* affairs we can draw neat—albeit artificial—boundaries. When is someone mature enough to marry or vote? Heaven only knows! But the law fixes that an arbitrary division be at eighteen or twenty-one years or whatever the jurisdiction determines. But in *theoretical* matters, neat boundaries cannot be fixed with acceptable precision. When is that ongoingly reconstructed ship "the same" rather than another; when is an artifact "a work of art" rather than a candidate for the shopping cart; when is a theory scientific rather than mere speculation? Such boundary questions are always intractable, and had the positivists been less doctrinarily closed-minded they might well have hung their hat on a more secure peg.

For another area where positivism encountered the largest obstacles was in relation to evaluative normativity. For observations can only ever reach that which is: the realm of what ought to be goes beyond its reach. Positivism was never able to come to convincing terms with issues of values and morality and for this reason never managed to make inroads among philosophers who engaged deeply with these realms of deliberation.

RELATED ANECDOTES

FURTHER READING

Ayer, A. J. *Language, Truth, and Logic.* New York: Dover, 1952.
Hempel, Carl G. "Problems and Changes in the Empiricist Criterion of Meaning." *Revue Internationale de Philosophie* 41 (1950): 41–46.
Jorgensen, Jorgen. *The Development of Logical Positivism.* Chicago: University of Chicago Press, 1951.
Passmore, John. *Philosophical Reasoning.* New York: Scribners, 1961.

87

POPPER'S FALSITY

RATIONAL INQUIRY HAS GENERALLY been characterized as the quest for truth. However, some thinkers have sought to turn this idea upside down by prioritizing not the attainment of truth but the avoidance of falsity.

Foremost is the Austro-British philosopher Karl R. Popper (1902–1994) who held that rational investigation, and scientific inquiry in particular, is a matter not of determining truth but of eliminating falsity:

> Science is not a system of certain, or well-established, statements; nor is it a system which steadily advances towards a state of finality. Our science is not knowledge (*epistémé*): it can never claim to have attained truth, or even a substitute for it, such as probability. . . . In Science we do not know: we can only guess. And our guesses are guided by the unscientific, the metaphysical (though biologically explicable) faith in laws, in regularities which we can uncover—discover. . . . Our method of research is not to defend them, in order to prove how right we were. On the contrary, we try to overthrow them. Using all the weapons of our logical, mathematical, and technical armoury we try to

prove that our anticipations were false—in order to put forward, in their stead, new unjustified and unjustifiable anticipations, new 'rash and premature prejudices,' as Bacon derisively called them.[1]

Seeing that science generally advances by way of later theories that supplement earlier, inadequate versions, Popper held the elimination of error to be the crux of inquiry and the detection of falsity as the pathway to progress.

Popper's position is reminiscent of Sherlock Holmes's elimination principle: "When you have eliminated all other possibilities, that which remains, however unlikely, must be the truth."

Despite its plausible appearance, however, this Popperian prioritization of falsity elimination has its problems. For only when we are dealing with a known finite range of collectively exhaustive possibilities are we bound to come any nearer to the truth as we eliminate incorrect possibilities. Whenever that range of possibilities is indeterminate—or even, for aught we know, infinite—in scope, elimination through falsification is a fruitless process that will get us no closer to the realities of the matter. In an artificial setting—like that of Agatha Christie's classic detective stories—eliminating suspects one at a time is bound to get us to the butler who did it. But with a real-life murderer on the streets of Chicago—let alone in seeing a remedy for the common cold—the business of one-at-a-time elimination is not a promising procedure.

As C. S. Peirce already stressed well before Popper, the elimination of falsehood will be of little use in the search for truth unless the elimination of incorrect answers increasingly narrows the field of yet open possibilities to those that are inherently more plausible and promising. Popper's falsificatist inquiry method requires the true answer to lie in a preidentified range of alternatives—a condition that all too readily goes unmet and is, in fact, virtually unmeetable in scientific matters where the truth is generally a needle in an unfathomable haystack.

---

1. Karl R. Popper, *The Logic of Scientific Discovery* (New York: Basic, 1969), 278–79.

RELATED ANECDOTES

FURTHER READING

Popper, Karl R. *The Logic of Scientific Discovery.* New York: Basic, 1969.
Rescher, Nicholas. *Peirce's Philosophy of Science.* Notre Dame: University of Notre Dame Press, 1978.

88

BOULDING'S MENACE

IN AN INTRIGUING 1965 paper titled "The Menace of Methuselah," Kenneth Boulding (1910–1993), an influential American economist, social theorist, and reformer, contemplated the social and economic implications of a substantially increased human life span. And here his analysis made it clear that what looks from the angle of individuals to be an unqualified plus—the increase in our expectation of life—can from the angle of society at large prove to be a decided negativity.

Specifically Boulding's thought proceeded along the following line: Let us suppose that the life expectancy of humans were somehow swiftly increased from roughly seventy to seven hundred years. What sort of securely predictable consequences would such a drastic lifespan elongation have for the society's social and, above all, economic arrangements? In pursuit of these deliberations Boulding examined such matters as:

- The crowding of human populations as the rate of departure from the world's stage is now diminished.
- The diminished scope for new talent as the productive life of geniuses and paragons becomes multiplied in length.

- The concentration of wealth under the impact of compound interest.

Through a host of examples of this sort, Boulding managed to justify the title of his paper by demonstrating that a vast array of clearly negative consequences would inevitably ensue from the substantial prolongation of life.

Boulding's speculation is highly illuminating for policy deliberations. For one thing, it serves to show that meaningful forays into social and political affairs always have to proceed systematically. The prospect of undesired results and collateral damage is often unavoidable in these matters. Changes designed "with the best of intentions" to fix one problem often can—and indeed generally will—produce undesirable results elsewhere. And the resultant balance of positivities and negativities should always be taken into careful account in societal innovation.

For another thing, Boulding's speculation manifests the value of "thinking outside the box." One would ordinarily incline to think that because we benignly regard longevity as a good thing, the more of it the better. But that Methuselah hypothesis clearly shows that this is by no means the case. Arrangements that on first sight might look to be desirable can have unexpected consequences that emphatically are not.

RELATED ANECDOTES

FURTHER READING

Boulding, Kenneth. "The Menace of Methuselah." *Journal of the Washington Academy of Sciences* 55 (1965): 171–79.
Rescher, Nicholas. "Why Isn't This a Better World?" *Reason and Religion*. Frankfurt: ONTOS, 2013.

89

AUSTIN'S VERBS

THE OXFORD PHILOSOPHER JOHN L. AUSTIN (1911–1960) was a leading member of the school of ordinary language philosophy, which sought to extract philosophical lessons from careful attention to how language is used by educated speakers in everyday communication. The guiding idea was that in philosophical deliberations, "we must pay attention to the facts of *actual* language, what we can and cannot say, and *precisely* why."[1]

Austin complained that philosophers are fixated upon factual assertions and claims to knowledge to the exclusion of the great variety of other things we do—and can do—with language. And accordingly he complained: "One thing, however, that it will be most dangerous to do, and that we are very prone to do, is to take it that we *somehow* know that the primary or primitive use of sentences must be, because it ought to be, statemental or constative, in the philosophers' preferred sense of simply uttering something whose sole pretension is to be true or false and which is not liable

---

1.   J. L Austin, *Philosophical Papers* (Oxford: Clarendon, 1961), 37.

to criticism in any other dimension. We certainly do not know that this is so."[2]

As Austin saw it, philosophical deliberations regarding language have become fixated upon its informative role to the neglect of other important language uses. And he complained that this has led philosophers into a quite inappropriate transition from acts of saying to "acts of knowing"—which are merely a linguistic (rather than optical) illusion. For—so Austin argued—there simply are no such things.

Thus consider that activities in which persons can engage are represented by possible answers to the question "What are you doing?" Here Austin stressed that there is an important contrast between verbs that can answer this question and verbs that cannot. Thus one can say: *I am engaged in*—

- running the race
- studying the calculus
- looking for my lost purse

But one cannot say: *I am engaged in*—

- winning the race
- understanding the calculus
- finding my lost purse

The former are *activities* that may well result in realizing the latter *states*, if pursued to a successful conclusion. But those states represent outcomes and not activities: they are not actions I am doing but the (possible) results thereof.

And Austin observed that just this is the case with knowing: it is not an activity but an end state, a possible outcome. In proper usage you cannot say "I am knowing that 2 + 2 = 4." You can be engaged in *learning* a fact but not in *knowing* it. The verb "to know" does not admit of a *present continuous* tense in correct English usage. And so to think and talk as though there is such a thing as an "act, action, or activity of knowing" is simply a grammatical deception. Knowledge is not a kind of activity but a possible end state in which various sorts of activities like investigating or learning or memo-

---

2.   J. L. Austin, *How to Do Things with Words* (Cambridge: Harvard University Press, 1962), 72.

rizing can result. Those theorists who deliberated about "acts of knowing" were simply barking up the wrong trees.

On the basis of such illustrations, Austin and his followers maintained philosophical confusion and error can often (and some extremists thought *always*) be averted by proper heed of the linguistic niceties.

RELATED ANECDOTES

1. The Tower of Babel 7
15. Plato's Knowledge 44

FURTHER READING

Austin, J. L. *How to Do Things with Words*. Cambridge: Harvard University Press, 1975.

Austin, J. L. *Philosophical Papers*. Oxford: Clarendon, 1961.

Urmson, J. O, et al. "J. L. Austin." In *The Linguistic Turn*. Edited by R. Rorty. Chicago: University of Chicago Press, 1967.

Warnock, G. J. *J. L. Austin*. London: Routledge, 1989.

AUSTIN'S EXCUSES

J. L. AUSTIN'S "A Plea for Excuses" is a classic attempt to extract philosophical lessons from careful heed to ordinary linguistic usage. Consider the following:

- When I return the money to the lender's identical twin, I do so "by mistake"—but one that is "only natural" and should be deemed virtually blameless.
- When I knock you down because I have slipped on a banana peel, I do so inadvertently "by accident" and am not at fault.

Many is the case when I blamelessly do something I should not do—and certainly would not do if the world were a more cooperative, user-friendly place.

But alas it is not. And there is no way to spell out in exhaustive detail all of the circumstances that might constitute an appropriate excuse for an unfortunate act. One cannot inventory all of those conceivably excusing conditions—there are just too many possibilities. I may be excused for failing to keep an appointment by "circumstances beyond my control," but it is also possible that I should have exercised due care in preventing these circumstances from arising.

And sometimes an otherwise valid excuse may fail to function. Here too Austin insisted that there is no adequate way to spell out in advance what this range of excuse-countervailing circumstances includes:

> To examine excuses is to examine cases where there has been some abnormality or failure: and as so often, the abnormal will throw light on the normal, will help us to penetrate the blinding veil of ease and obviousness that hides the mechanisms of the natural successful act. It rapidly becomes plain that the breakdowns signalised by the various excuses are of radically different kinds, affecting different parts or stages of the machinery, which the excuses consequently pick out and sort out for us.[1]

The conclusion Austin proposed to draw from a close attention to usage is that in matters of the appropriateness and inappropriateness of actions there is no prospect to achieving full and comprehensive detail, and there is no hope of finding explicit rules of algorithmic precision.

Foremost among the larger lessons here is the fact that there is an indispensable need for good judgment in matters of ethics. The rules and principles at work here (and so prized by rigoristic theoreticians such as Kant) are in the end no more than guidelines whose appropriate implementation requires sense and sensibility.

RELATED ANECDOTES

2. Aesop's Donkey   11
52. Kant's Errand Boy   153
93. Simon's Satisficing   260

FURTHER READING

Austin, J. L. "A Plea for Excuses." *Proceedings of the Aristotelian Society* 57 (1956–1957): 1–30

Statman, Daniel, ed. *Moral Luck*. Albany: SUNY Press, 1993.

---

1.   J. L. Austin, "A Plea for Excuses," *Proceedings of the Aristotelian Society* 57 (1956–1957): 5–6.

91

TURING'S TEST

CAN MACHINES THINK? An interesting question! But before addressing it, one had best ask another: Just what is it that betokens the presence of thought? By what standard are we to judge that thinking is at work and that an intelligent being would be at issue with an ingenious product of scientific artifice?

The English logician, mathematician, and cryptanalyst Alan Turning (1912–1954) proposed a simple-sounding test here. As he saw it, we should be prepared to credit machines with intelligence if and when we cannot distinguish in interrogatory situations between their operation and that of humans. The resulting Turing test procedure is thus straightforward: Play a question-and-answer dialogue with the interlocutor. If and when there is no (dialogue-internal) way of telling whether it is a human being or a machine that is responding, that interlocutor should be acknowledged as an intelligent being.

But is this a reasonable test?

It is by now transparently clear that in answering questions about advisable chess moves, computers can do every bit as well as humans. Moreover, suppose that the question agenda included a request for information of the sort that could be found in a reference book—a dictionary, say, or an encyclopedia or almanac. Since all this sort of thing could be programmed into a computer's search-accessible memory, there would presumably be no possible way to tell the nature of our respondent—except perhaps via superior performance! (After all, "to err is human.") Clearly there is an impressive range of human things a computer can also do as well as we ourselves—or even better. But at what point does such performance establish actual thinking?

Suppose we ask our respondent about its own activities: Will you answer all my questions truthfully? Will you be answering further questions tomorrow? Will you answer the next question I will pose to you affirmatively? Again as long as lying is an available option, there will here too be no ready way to distinguish the sort of interlocutor at issue, a thinking being or a cleverly programmed automaton.

Apparently, if there indeed is a difference in intelligent performance between humans and machines, the Turing test is just not strong enough to detect it. Something more challenging might well be needed. But what more—over and above question-and-answer exchanges—could invariably be required?

One possibility might be to shift from verbal to performatory responses, shifting from factual questions to instructions. The problem with the Turing test seems to lie in the overly intellectualized, purely textual nature of its procedure. To qualify as an artificially intelligent being—a being whose proceedings are grounded by actual thought—one seemingly has to monitor not just verbal but also actually manipulative behavior: not just texts but actions. Perhaps verbalization is simply not enough and intelligent *agency* is requisite for thinking. The capacity to respond intelligently at the level of matter-of-fact interrogation may well not be adequate for establishing the credentials of thought in the way one would expect for intelligent beings. For, given the limitations of language, questions will have a restricted and well-defined inventory of possible answers, whereas the range of possible responses at the behavioral level can prove to be potentially open-ended and unlimited.

RELATED ANECDOTES

FURTHER READING

Cooper, C. B., and Jan Van Leeuwen, eds. *Alan Turing: His Work and Impact*. New York: Elsevier, 2013.

Leavitt, David. *The Man Who Knew Too Much: Alan Turing and the Invention of the Computer*. New York: W. W. Norton, 2006.

92

URMSON'S APPLES

THE OXFORD PHILOSOPHER J. O. Urmson (1915–2012) is usually classed as a member of the school of ordinary language philosophy, although he himself never endorsed a particular method of understanding, believing that "the philosopher sees what needs doing and does it." One of the things Urmsom thought needed doing was defending the rationality of evaluation in opposing those who, like A. J. Ayer and the logical positivists, saw it as meaningless verbiage or who, like the University of Michigan's C. L. Stevenson, saw it as a purely personal "matter of taste" preferentialism, with "x has value" as amounting to "I approve of X."

Urmson set out to refute this value nihilism not via general principles but by a concrete example, a case study. And for this end he focused on something simple and commonplace: apples. Their evaluation, he stressed, is not baseless and arbitrary: there are definite grounding standards set by agriculturists for establishing the quality grade of different kinds of apples, classing them at various quality levels (super or extra fancy and so on). Accordingly the ground for his deliberations was not seeded by the speculation of some philosopher but by the regulations for the Ministry of Agriculture and Fisheries for grading and packing apples. Throughout this range there are factually determinate characteristics—accessible to observation and inspection—that afford quality-determinative criteria. And these cognitively cogent and commonly accepted standards provide for the meaningful and informative evaluation of the quality of apples. And the same sorts of processes are at work in adjudging quality in flower shows, in dog shows, and the like. Thus as Urmson saw it: "Grading statements being, as I maintain, objectively decidable, they are, for many reasons, more important and impressive than mere indications of personal likes and dislikes. [For this very reason] we therefore tend to use them [even] when all we are really entitled to do is to state our likes and dislikes."[1]

And so, Urmson contended, those theorists who adopt a dismissively subjectivistic position in matters of evaluative assessment simply ignore the realities of actual practice. In their blind adherence to their doctrinal ideology value skeptics ignore the fact that evaluation is not an idiosyncratic and feckless procedure but a rational process that does—or should—be subject to contextually cogent rules. And Urmson viewed this situation as particularly prominent in ethical and moral matters:

> Resistance to recognising the ordinary grading mechanism as operating in morals is set up by the undoubted fact that moral grading is so much more important; we feel so much more strongly about the attainment of high moral grades than others. Being a good cricketer is excellent in its way, but not vital; being a good citizen, a good father, a good man, is very different. This creates the impression that to call someone a good man is logically different from calling him a good cricketer. The one point I shall make about this is that in grading people in non-moral matters and in grading things we are dealing with dispensable qualifications in people and dispensable things. But moral grade affects the whole of one's life and social intercourse—a low grade in this makes other high gradings unimportant.[2]

1. J. O. Urmson, "On Grading," *Mind* 59 (1950): 163.
2. Urmson, "On Grading," 168.

Viewed in this light, evaluation plays a significant and appropriate role in human affairs. And Urmson argued that it does so on an essentially factual and empirical basis, reflecting the natural response of human beings in situations where their interests are at stake.

RELATED ANECDOTES

FURTHER READING

Dancy, Jonathan, et al., eds. *Human Agency: Language, Duty, and Value*. Stanford: Stanford University Press, 1988.

Urmson, J. O. *The Emotive Theory of Ethics*. London: Hutchinson, 1968.

Urmson, J. O. "On Grading." *Mind* 59 (1950): 145–69.

93

SIMON'S SATISFICING

ECONOMISTS ARE GENERALLY EXTREMALISTS: for most of them, the name of the game is maximizing (for example, cost-effectiveness) or minimizing (for example, effort). But the American information theorist and Nobel-winning economist Herbert Simon (1916–2001) proved to be the crucial exception here. He propounded the idea that real-life decision makers do not strive for optimal and maximally effective solutions but rather *satisficed* ones in opting for solutions that are merely good enough to meet the needs of the situation. Where others saw economic rationality as requiring an optimization striving for the realizable best, Simon saw as critical a *bounded rationality* that settles for what is good enough for the purposes at hand.

There is a great deal of practical good sense to this approach. And there is much truth in the proverb that the best is the enemy of the good. For in striving for an unattainable perfection, people often lose out on more realistic opportunities for improving matters. Thus in matters of choice where no solution will possibly please everyone, one does well to opt for an alternative that will cause the least distress.

This situation is readily illustrated in voting processes. Thus let four individuals (*A–D*) indicate their preference-order among four alternatives (*I–IV*).

	I	*II*	*III*	*IV*
A	1	4	3	2
B	4	1	3	2
C	4	3	1	2
D	1	3	4	2

Clearly no solution is optimal here—no matter which alternative is adopted not everyone will get their first choice. With each of alternatives *I–III* there will be at least two people who are seriously disgruntled with bottom-ranked (3 or 4) results. But with alternative *IV*, while no one is delighted (gets choice 1), no one is gravely dissatisfied by a 4-rated result. So everyone is well advised to "settle" by accepting second best and resting content with that which, while decidedly suboptimal, is "good enough in the circumstances."

Simon's idea of accepting local adequacy can find constructive application in philosophy itself. For it can demotivate the hoary but vain philosophical search for a global *summum bonum:* a supreme good. After all, a quest for "the good life" can and doubtless should take the sensible line of looking to modes of life that are good enough rather than seeking the single one that is supremely best.

RELATED ANECDOTES

FURTHER READING

Kahneman, Daniel, Paul Slovik, and Amos Tversky. *Judgment under Uncertainty.* Cambridge: Cambridge University Press, 1982.

Simon, Herbert. *Reason in Human Affairs.* Stanford: Stanford University Press, 1983.

94

THE PRISONER'S DILEMMA

IN THE LATE 1940S the mathematicians Merrill Flood (1908–1991) and Melvin Dresher (1911–1992) of the RAND think tank in California framed a problem in decision theory to which the Princeton mathematician A. W. Tucker (1905–1995) subsequently gave the format (and the name) of a "prisoner's dilemma." It envisions the situation of two now separated but then collaborating culprits caught up in a situation where if neither confesses, only a minor charge can be proved against them, while if both confess, a heavy penalty will be imposed. But if one has state's evidence and the other not, then the confessor's sentence will be substantially lighter. The resultant situation will thus look as per table 1.

Table 1. Probable prison sentences for prisoners *A* and *B* (in years of incarceration)

	B Confesses	*B does not confess*
A confesses	5/5	1/6
A does not confess	6/1	2/2

Note: An entry *a/b* indicates a sentence of *a* years for *A* and *b* years for *B*.

Here A reasons on standard decision-theoretic principles of safety-first prudence: "If I confess, then whichever way B may choose, I'll be better off than I otherwise would be." And B of course will reason similarly. So our culprits will arrive at what is clearly a suboptimal result for both of them, losing the opportunity to reach a mutually much-preferable result.

Another possible approach—one based on a consideration of probabilities—also seems promising. Let it be that A assesses the probability of B's confessing as p. But now consider table 2. Here no matter how A actually assesses the probability p of B's confessing, himself confessing once more affords him what appears as the better outcome, and so from the angle of expectation, mutual confession looks to be the prudentially sensible course.

Table 2. The expected result for A (in years of incarceration)

	B confesses	B does not confess	Expectation
A confesses	$5p$	$1(1-p)$	$4p+1$
A does not confess	$6p$	$2(1-p)$	$4p+2$

There is clearly a paradox here. By doing "the rationally advisable thing" our two prisoners lose out on an available result that is clearly superior and mutually preferable.

There is, however, yet another, different way of looking at it. For A might reason as follows: Let us suppose that the problem has a rational resolution—which after all, is what is being asked for. Since my opponent is in exactly the same position as I myself, this will have to be identical for the two of us. So both of us will act exactly alike. But this leaves only two possibilities, of which not confessing is obviously the superior. This perspective too looks altogether sensible.

Clearly there are different lines of seemingly rational approach, in particular, one (play-safe self-proposition) that is primarily outcome-oriented and another (rationality-oriented) primarily process-oriented. From a theoretician's standpoint, they unfortunately lead to divergent results. So in the final analysis there is no decisively correct resolution here. The choice will depend on the chooser's experience-based orientation to decide whether priority of emphasis is to be given to the all-too-common egocentrism or to the somewhat idealized rationality of people.

The example conveys the instructive lesson that there are very different perfectly "rational" ways of approaching the issue, specifically those based on safety-first prudence, symmetry considerations, and probabilism. The choice among the alternatives before one transcends into a second-order choice: What sort of approach is to be employed in trying to resolve the issue at hand? Abstract considerations of theoretical rationality cannot resolve the problem of which perspective to adopt. The issue is one of harmonization between the specific situation at hand and the theoretical procedures available for its resolution.

RELATED ANECDOTES

FURTHER READING

Axelrod, Robert. *The Evolution of Cooperation*. New York: Basic, 1984.

Harrington, Joseph E. *Games, Strategies, and Decision Making*. New York: Worth, 2009.

Howard, Nigel. *Paradoxes of Rationality*. Cambridge: MIT Press, 1971.

Poundstone, William. *Prisoner's Dilemma*. New York: Anchor, 1992.

Rapoport, A., and A. M. Chammah. *Prisoner's Dilemma*. Ann Arbor: University of Michigan Press, 1965.

Williams, J. D. *The Complete Strategist*. Santa Monica: RAND, 1954.

95

A STREETCAR NAMED DISASTER

IN A 1967 ARTICLE, the English philosopher Philippa Foot (1920–2010) posed a widely discussed ethical conundrum that ran essentially as follows:

> You are standing by the side of a track when you see a runaway streetcar hurtling toward you. Clearly the driver has lost control. Ahead are five people, tied to the track. If you do nothing, the five will be run over and killed. Fortunately you are next to a signal switch: turning this switch will send the out-of-control vehicle down a side track, a spur, just ahead of you. But there is a snag: on the spur you spot one person tied to the track. Diverting the streetcar will inevitably result in this person being killed. What should you do?[1]

The streetcar situation offers a choice between two unpleasant alternatives. The alternatives are *to act* or *not to act*, to divert or not to divert. The respective outcomes are as per table 1.

---

1. Adapted from David Edmunds, *Would You Kill the Fat Man* (Princeton: Princeton University Press, 2013), 9. Foot's example approach originally in the *Oxford Review* 5 (1967). It figured prominently in her *Virtues and Vices*.

Table 1. To act or not to act		
	Consequence	
	For the world	*For the agent*
Inaction	several lives lost	freedom from causal responsibility for this outcome
Action	a single life lost	bearing the causal responsibility for this outcome

Here the operative question is: Is an agent morally obligated to assume causal responsibility for a bad outcome in order to prevent one that is yet worse for the overall scheme of things? In sum: Does the injunction "minimize harm" constitute a moral obligation? If it does not, then the agent can refrain from acting and walk away with the ever-popular reaction: "It's not *my* responsibility." If it does, then of course our agent is obligated to divert and thereby bear causal responsibility for the unhappy outcome.

In the ethical tradition of the West, most ethical systems—be they Christian, Kantian, or utilitarian—accept harm minimization as a paramount obligation. And on this basis, our agent should regretfully divert, assuming the guilt of causal responsibility as a cross that a moral agent has to bear in an imperfect world. But on a variant ethics of do no harm, maintain clean hands prioritization, our agent would have "to let nature take its course."

And of course the problem admits of endless variations. What if instead of those five people we had a bomb killing a thousand? Or what if the choice were between a young priest and an old pedophile? Many ethical considerations can come into play in the variations of Foot's vexing thought experiment.

RELATED ANECDOTES

FURTHER READING

Cathcart, Thomas. *The Trolley Problem, or, Would You Throw the Fat Guy Off the Bridge? A Philosophical Conundrum.* New York: Workman, 2013.

Edmonds, David. *Would You Kill the Fat Man?* Princeton: Princeton University Press, 2013.

Foot, Philippa. *Virtues and Vices.* Oxford: Blackwell, 1978.

96

PUTNAM'S TWIN EARTH

THE IDEA OF A Twin Earth was projected in a 1973 paper by the Harvard philosopher Hilary Putnam (1926–) to make a far-reaching point in the philosophy of language. In effect, his example is based on the following supposition: Imagine a hypothetical planet, Twin Earth, just like the Earth but with one salient difference, namely, that what is universally acknowledged as "water" on Twin Earth (filling its lakes, storage tanks, bathtubs, and so on) is actually not H_2O but some other like-water-behaving stuff W. Then it is clear that by "water" those Twin Earth inhabitants do actually mean something else (namely, W). But what they actually think and say about "water" is for all of them (possibly excepting chemists during their professional hours) substantially the same as what we think and say on the matter.

This being the case—so Putnam argued—"water" means something else on Twin Earth and therefore *meaning* is not something subjective (something that "lies in the head") but is a matter of the objective reality of things. For what goes on in the thought life of those Twin Earth denizens is (or may be presumed to be) the same as what goes on with us when discussing water. But something else is in fact at issue: they *think* of water as we do, but they *refer* to something quite different. And as Putnam sees it, objective reference trumps thought-determined meaning.

Plausible though this sounds, there is a problem. The hitch is that it is neither difficult nor implausible to turn the matter on its head, holding that while this *referent* differs from ours, the *meaning* is the same. For while Putnam has it that meaning is independent of thought and determined by reference, one could just as well invert the reasoning and maintain that meaning is independent of reference and determined by thought. In Fregean terms the issue is simply whether it is sense (*Sinn*) or reference (*Bedeutung*) that is to be seen as the paramount determiner of "meaning." And so it could be maintained without anomaly that Twin Earth people sense-*mean* by water just what we do, but that, owing to contingent features of their environment, it so happens that they *refer* to something else with this terminology.

It can, however, also be argued that if one were to shift the level of considerations from an entire society to a particular individual, then Putnam's point that "meaning is not in the head" is well taken. For the meaning of terms is clearly not a matter of potentially idiosyncratic personal conviction but of societally established norms.

And so with even as simple seeming an issue as that regarding what words mean, careful reflection indicates a complex gearing of wheels within wheels.

RELATED ANECDOTES

FURTHER READING

Davidson, Mathew, ed. *On Sense and Direct Reference: Readings in the Philosophy of Language*. Boston: McGraw-Hill, 2007.

Pessin, Andrew, and Sanford Goldberg, eds. *The Twin Earth Chronicles*. Armonk: M. E. Sharpe, 1996.

Putnam, Hilary. "The Meaning of Meaning." *Mind, Language, and Reality*. Cambridge: Cambridge University Press, 1975. Reprints his paper "Meaning and Reference," *Journal of Philosophy* 70 (1973): 197–211, in which the Twin Earth thought experiment originated.

97

DR. PSYCHO'S PRESCRIPTION

THE PRESENT AUTHOR'S DR. PSYCHO paradox affords yet another instructive example of the intricacies of rational decision.[1] Consider the problem posed by a somewhat eccentric friend of yours, Dr. Psychic Psycho, an otherwise intelligent, serious, reliable, and generally sagacious and self-assured biochemist who fancies himself a clairvoyant psychic and actually has a good track record for oddball predictions. After you have just eaten apples together, he proceeds to astonish you with the following announcement:

> I have interesting news for you. You must seriously consider taking this pill. As you know (since we have recently determined it together), it contains substance X, which as you also know (but consult this pharmacopoeia if in doubt) is fatally poisonous by itself while nevertheless furnishing unfailing antidote to poison Z—though it does have some minorly unpleasant side effects. Now the apple I gave to you, which you have just finished eating,

1. On this problem, see the author's "Predictive Incapacity and Rational Decision," *European Review* 3 (1995): 325–30.

was poisoned by me with Z—or not—in line with my prediction as to your taking or not taking the antidote pill. Benign old me of course only poisoned the apple if I foresaw that you were indeed going to take the antidote. And not to worry—as you know, I'm a very good predictor.[2]

At this point your strange friend rushes off and vanishes from the scene. Any prospect of forcing the truth out of him disappears with his departure. And an awful feeling comes over you—you cannot but believe him. In fact, you strongly suspect that he went through the whole rigmarole to get you to take that problem pill. What do you do? Your very life seems to depend on predicting the result of taking that pill.

Of course you proceed to do a quick bit of decision theoretic calculation. For starters, you map out the spectrum of available possibilities per table 1.

Table 1. Alternatives with Dr. Psycho's choices

You	He predicts	According to him, you	Your system contains	Result?
take	correctly	take	Z, X	survive
take	incorrectly	not take	X	die
not take	correctly	not take	neither	survive
not take	incorrectly	take	Z	die

Not a pretty picture. After all, you stand a chance of dying whether or not you take that accursed pill. What to do?

Note that no matter what you do, the same basic situation occurs. If he predicts correctly, you survive; if he predicts incorrectly, you die. Since nothing you do has any effect on the outcome (which depends entirely on his competence as a predictor and thus on circumstances you can neither control nor influence), it doesn't matter what you do.

The fact of it is that sometimes rational analysis *underdetermines* the choice of an advisable resolution: there are no telling arguments

2. See Nicholas Rescher, *Paradoxes* (Chicago: Open Court, 2001), 269–75.

for selecting one possibility over or against some other alternative. And the present situation is, as it were, a cousin to that one. In both cases alike it becomes impossible to say with warranted confidence how even an ideally rational agent would proceed. In such a case there is not rational help for it: "you pays your money and you takes your chance."

But in the present case there is another aspect to it. For there is always the possibility that the doctor is lying—that the only thing he did with the apple is to tell a fictitious tale about it. Then you have nothing to gain by taking that pill. So all considered you had best let things stand, hoping that the good doctor is either a liar or a genius.

RELATED ANECDOTES

FURTHER READING

Campbell, Richmond, and Lanning Sowden. *Paradoxes of Rationality and Co-operation: Prisoner's Dilemma and Newcomb's Problem*. Vancouver: University of British Columbia Press, 1985.

Rescher, Nicholas. *Paradoxes*. Chicago: Open Court, 2001.

98

VAGRANT PREDICATES

MANY LOGICIANS STAND COMMITTED to the so-called intuitionist doctrine that something of a certain description can properly be claimed to exist only when one can actually provide an instantiating example of this. And building on this idea, various positivistically inclined metaphysicians assert that existential claims are only appropriate where substantiating instances can be adduced. There is, however, a serious impediment in the way of this "show me" approach, namely, the frailty and weakness of the human intellect and the limited scope of our knowledge.

The fact of it is that an item can be referred to obliquely in such a way that, as a matter of principle, any and all prospect of its specific identification is precluded. This phenomenon is illustrated by claims to the (clearly unquestionable) existence of

> a thing whose identity will never be known
> a fact that has never occurred to anybody
> a person whom everyone has nowadays utterly forgotten
> an occurrence that no one has ever mentioned
> an integer that is never individually specified

Such items certainly exist. But they are *identificationally inaccessible*: to indicate them concretely and specifically as bearers of the predicate at issue is straightaway to unravel them as so-characterized items.

We can, of course, discuss such individuals at large and even to some extent describe them, but what we cannot do is to *identify* them. They elude the reach of specificity. Their cognitive inaccessibility is built into the very specification at issue, as with:

> being a grain of sand that no one ever took note of
> being a person who has passed into total oblivion
> being a never-formulated question
> being an idea no one mentions any longer

To identify such an item would automatically unravel its specifying characterization. Such predicates are "vagrant" in the sense of *having no known address or fixed abode*. Despite their having applications, these cannot be specifically instanced—they cannot be housed in a particular spot.

In the context of the present deliberations, one must face the prospect that the present "optimal possible world" is a vagrant predicate in that, while it is plausible to assure that there is (or might well be) such a thing, nevertheless, neither this world nor any other definitely specifiable alternative to it can be claimed to qualify as bearer of this predication.

Vagrant predicates betoken the unavoidability of areas of ignorance and unknowability. In this regard they are emblematic of the fact that one of the most critical but yet problematic areas of inquiry relates to knowledge regarding our own cognitive shortcomings. To be sure there is no problem with the idea that Q is a question that we cannot answer. But it is impossible to get a more definite fix on our own ignorance, because we cannot know what that correct answer is that is unknown to us. It is not just in philosophy but in everyday life that we must be prepared to spread the wings of thought over things that have to be accepted "sight unseen" without our being able to confront them accurately for closer scrutiny.

RELATED ANECDOTES

FURTHER READING

Rescher, Nicholas. *Epistemic Logic*. Pittsburgh: University of Pittsburgh Press, 2005.
Rescher, Nicholas. *Unknowability*. Lanham: Rowman and Littlefield, 2009.

99

SEARLE'S CHINESE ROOM

COGNITIVE THEORISTS OFTEN HOLD that to know a fact is to be able to give correct answers to questions about it. But this plausible idea does not work. Consider the following question-and-answer exchanges.

> Q: When will Jones arrive here?
> A: When he gets here.
> Q: When next will it rain?
> A: The next time raindrops fall from the sky.
> Q: What is the square root of 2?
> A: That number which, when multiplied by itself, yields 2 as a product.

In these and all other such cases, the response is quite correct but nowise informative. Accordingly, the ability to provide correct answers to questions is not necessarily indicative of substantive *knowledge*. And extending this idea yet further, the American philosopher John Searle (1932–) gave a telling argument to the effect that the ability to provide correct answers to questions is not even necessarily indicative of *understanding*:

Imagine that I, a non-Chinese speaker, am locked in a room with a lot of Chinese symbols in boxes. I am given an instruction book in English for matching Chinese symbols with other Chinese symbols and for giving back bunches of Chinese symbols in response to bunches of Chinese symbols put into the room through a small window. Unknown to me, the symbols put in through the window are called questions. The symbols I give back are called answers to the questions. The boxes of symbols I have are called a database, and the instruction book in English is called a program. The people who give me questions and designed the instruction book are called the programmers, and I am called the computer. We imagine that I get so good at shuffling the symbols, and the programmers get so good at writing the program, that eventually my "answers" to the "questions" are indistinguishable from those of a native Chinese speaker; I pass the Turing test for understanding Chinese. But all the same, I don't understand a word of Chinese.[1]

The "perfect translator" who can answer correctly all questions of the format "Does sentence I_1 in language L_1 mean the same as I_2 in language L_2" is one who has mastered the relationships among symbolisms. Issues of the format "How would you say in *your* language what I_1 means in L_1" may still be totally beyond this translator. And any and all questions of the format "If I_1 in L_1 were true—if, for example, it were the case that the French statement 'Cette femme là vous deteste' were true—what sort of response on your part would be in order?" might still leave the translator baffled in the absence of a considerable body of contextual information.

So *understanding* clearly involves more than linguistic manipulation. (In this regard the pragmatists have it right.) For what would appear to be crucial for intelligent understanding is not the mere ability to provide correct answers as such but the management of a procedure or method by which the (actual or at least probable) correctness of those answers can be established: in sum it is *process* rather than *product* that is of the essence here.

---

1.   John Searle in Samuel Guttenpan, ed., *A Companion to the Philosophy of Mind* (Oxford: Blackwell, 1994), 546.

RELATED ANECDOTE

FURTHER READING

Searle, John. *Consciousness and Language.* Cambridge: Cambridge University Press, 2002.

Searle, John. *Minds, Brains, and Science.* Cambridge: Harvard University Press, 1984.

100

THE BELL CURVE'S SLANT

THE 1994 BOOK BY Herrnstein and Murray on *The Bell Curve* achieved an imposing success by scandal.[1] For its deliberations pivoted on one prime consideration that ran roughly as follows: There is a statistical discrepancy in IQ test results between whites and blacks that evidences a discrepant capacity to benefit for training and education. The fact, however, is that any close inspection of the matter shows that this bugaboo of horrendous consequences is a very dubious proposition. To bring this to light clearly, it is useful to consider a case of substantially the same structure that carries a far lower emotional charge.

The comparison case that is worth pondering is that of the male-female divide in the context of longevity. Let us take it as conceded—as is surely plausible on the presently available evidence—that the life expectancy of males and females represents a desirable feature that is, moreover, measurable, biologically determined, and significantly unresponsive to (further) social policy manipulation

1. Richard J. Herrnstein and Charles Murray, *The Bell Curve: Intelligence and Class Structure in American Life* (New York: Free, 1994).

in already advanced technological societies. And let it further be granted that—as all the available evidence indicates—women are advantaged over men in point of this particular asset, with only one man in three or four surviving the average lifespan for females. Does this situation of itself warrant any conclusions whatsoever as regards the institution of social policies that bear differentially on the interests of men and women?

Consider the possibilities. Does the existence of a bell-curve discrepancy in life expectancy as between men and women imply that society should invest more in providing for the health of men than in providing for the health of women? Does it mean that, since men have fewer years to enjoy life's benefits, something should be done to advantage them in some compensatory way? Does it mean that, since women have more inactive years per year of productive life than men do, their annual claims upon socially distributed benefits are diminished? The answer here is clearly: *None of the above.* The fact that women live longer than men in and of itself has no implication whatsoever for how the goods or bads of a society should be distributed between them. It is—or should be—perfectly clear that in the case of the differential longevity of men and women, there just are no valid public policy considerations that would unfairly advantage the one group as against the other. Whether you are an egalitarian who wants to have everyone treated just alike or a chauvinist who thinks that one group should be advantaged over the other—either way, that bell-curve discrepancy in and of itself does nothing to aid or injure your cause.

An important lesson here relates to what might be termed the principle of thematic homogeneity in the theory of rational inference. The principle has the following format: if a cogent inference is to yield a conclusion of a certain type as output, then the premises must also afford inputs of this same type.

This principle applies directly in the present case. Statistics are a matter of purely factual reportage. So if a parting conclusion is to emerge, there must be substantively committed policy premises over and above these statistical reports that can carry the probative weight of the argumentation.

In and of themselves, such statistical disparities have no policy implications. Only in conjunction with what is itself a substantial policy principle—be it explicit or implicit, tacit or overt—can they provide for policy implications. They can only function as minor premises in arguments with a policy major. And then it will be that policy major that carries the weight and does the real work. No socially adverse conclusions can validly be drawn from the Herrnstein-Murray statistics themselves.

RELATED ANECDOTES

72. Durkheim's Suicides   204
88. Boulding's Menace   247

FURTHER READING

Rescher, Nicholas. "The Bell Curve Revisited." *Public Affairs Quarterly* 9 (1995): 321–30.

DERRIDA'S DEMOLITION

THE FRENCH PHILOSOPHER JACQUES DERRIDA (1930–2004) is best known for devising a method of text analysis that has become known as deconstruction. No small part of his notoriety is due to the deliberately contrived obscurity of his writing (and doubtless of his thought as well).

Concealment by language is the watchword here. Thus Derrida writes:

> The primordial sexual difference is tender, gentle, peaceful; when that difference is struck down by a "curse" . . . the duality or the duplicity of the two becomes unleashed, indeed bestial, opposition. . . . This schema would come under neither metaphysical theology nor explicable theology. But the premordality (pre-Platonic, pre-metaphysical or pre-Christian) to which Heidegger recalls us . . . *has no other content and even other language* than that of Platonism and Christianity. This primordality is simply that starting from which things like metaphysics and Christianity are possible and thinkable. But that constitutes their arch-morning origin and their ultra-Occidental

horizon is nothing other than this hollow of a repetition, in the strongest and most unusual sense of this term.[1]

Just what this means, and what the point is, is largely "left as an exercise for the reader"—and many academics are happy to respond to the challenge.

Derrida's position was already incorporated in Talleyrand's famous dictum that "speech was given to man for disguising his thought." For what is at issue is in effect a conspiracy theory of discourse. Applying this principle to the analysis of texts, the aim of deconstruction is not to elucidate, to clarify, to make explicit but rather to suggest concealed meanings, hidden agendas. Where text is concerned, it is less what is on the printed page that matters than what is hidden from view, suggested, implied, hinted at. The unity of deconstruction is to find in the text that which its author seeks to conceal—and is perhaps even not consciously aware of.

The conflict between deconstructionists and their critics thus reflects a deep divergence of view about the role of texts in communication. And at this point the text no longer belongs to its author but to its interpreters. Where analytic philosophers sought to find truth in the details of discourse, what the devotees of deconstruction see themselves as finding is largely misunderstanding and self-delusion, and insofar as such a theory of philosophical discourse holds good, we are brought back to the starting point of the Tower of Babel story.

RELATED ANECDOTES

FURTHER READING

Norris, Christopher. *Derrida*. Cambridge: Harvard University Press, 1987.
Sallis, John, ed. *Deconstruction and Philosophy: The Texts of Jacques Derrida*. Chicago: University of Chicago Press, 1987.

---

1. Jacques Derrida, "Geschlecht II," in *Deconstruction and Philosophy*, ed. J. Sallis (Chicago: University of Chicago Press, 1987), 193.

INDEX OF NAMES

Note: when individuals are the subject of an anecdote, they and the subsequent anecdote page references will appear in **boldface**.